Marketing Fusion

Marketing Strategies to Scale Your Business

Matt Booher
Jodi Brandstetter
Dan Hahn
Kendra Ramirez
Peg Stookey
Kimberlee Vollbrecht

Melanie Booher
Katy Crossen
Margaret Moore
Katie Scanlon
James Szuch
Janice Weiser

Influence Network Media

Influence Network Media, LLC

Copyright @ 2022 Influence Network Media, LLC

All Rights Reserved. Apart from any fair dealing for purposes of research or private study, or criticism or review, as permitted under the Copyright, Designs and Patents Act 1988, this publication may only be reproduced, stored or transmitted, in any form or by any means, with the prior permission in writing of the copyright owner, or in the case of the reprographic reproduction in accordance with the terms of licenses issued by the Copyright Licensing Agency. Enquires concerning reproduction outside those terms should be sent to the publisher.

Contents

	Introduction	1
1.	Marketing Strategy Blueprint	5
	Kendra Ramirez	19
2.	The Touchy-Feely Truth About Marketing	21
	Katy Crossen	35
3.	Build Your Brand of Brilliance	37
	Peg Stookey	63
4.	Treasured Products	67
	James Szuch	93
5.	Tell Your Story and Market Your Business 21 Ways	95
	Margee Moore and Janice Weiser	119
6.	The 7 Key Pieces Of The Digital Marketing Puzzle	121
	Dan Hahn	141
7.	Getting Started with Digital Analytics and Dashboards	145
	Matt Booher	163
8.	Pipeline Plumbing	165
	Kimberlee Vollbrecht	179
9.	Relationship Networking and Marketing	181
	Katie Scanlon	189
10.	One Chapter, One Bio and A Headshot	191
	Jodi Brandstetter	201
	Conclusion	203
	Melanie Booher	205

About Influence Network Media	207
Business Fusion Book Series	211
Women of Business Book Series	213
Influence Network Media Multi-Author Book Services	215
Book Smarts Business Podcast	217

Introduction

Worst. Grades. Ever.

Yes, my worst grades in college were not so proudly achieved in Marketing.

I remember thinking that marketing would be the easiest of college courses (Really, how difficult could people, price, and promotion be?!), and I eagerly signed up for a variety of Marketing courses within my business program. For a fleeting moment, I even considered majoring in Marketing. After all, it sounded so much easier than Finance, Economics, Accounting, Organizational Development, or Management Information Systems. Boy, was I wrong!

As an entrepreneur and business owner, I started off as many do – gungho and ready to take on the world. I'd do it all myself. A one-woman show. I started with my own strategic, financial, operations, and marketing plans and was eager to grow my business.

Other entrepreneurs know how this story shapes up – surprise – it didn't work. I dabbled in all the startup areas, trying to do it all myself. I was so overwhelmed that I wasn't able to focus on the core nature of my business. Each day was stressful and left me generally unfulfilled.

My business had a marketing dilemma. The options were overwhelming and complex, with so many fields of expertise. Even if I honed my networking skills, could I also excel at blogging? Did I need a better website or SEO? How does one create a successful marketing strategy? Should I use a CRM, sales funnel, or dashboards? So many questions.

With all of this in mind, I knew what had to be done. I had to learn to share the load, delegate and streamline for efficiency by getting those involved who know their craft better than I ever would. Good news – I've been blessed to cross paths with exceptional Marketing leaders over the course of my career. The universe must have known that I'd need their expertise to make up for my shortcomings in the matter!

Marketing plays an integral role in business, and the need for expertise grows as your business changes. There is a multitude of disciplines within marketing and many are difficult to master. And that my friends, is the brilliance of this book.

We've gathered some of the brightest Marketing minds to create Marketing Fusion – writing amazing chapters and sharing expertise related to their craft. Years of learning, trying new methods, advancing new technologies, and serving clients – all collected here so that you can choose which area might make the most sense for your organization. And the best news – they're sharing it with you!

This book is not meant to be an all-encompassing Marketing book, we don't have enough pages for that! However, if you are seeking some fresh perspective from leaders who have seen success in their field – this book is for you. Or maybe you are looking for new ideas to freshen up your stale marketing plan and springboard your organization into the 21st-century? Marketing Fusion will spur innovation and ideas for an improved marketing strategy within your organization.

The leaders of this book possess knowledge in critical areas including digital analytics and dashboards, overall Marketing strategy, LinkedIn expertise and utilization, the importance of sales funnels, networking and referral marketing, the power of storytelling, really listening to clients' stories by tapping into empathy in order to better serve customers and potential clients, SEO, and blogging.

Each chapter educates on a different discipline and offers ideas to raise existing marketing efforts to a new level. We encourage you to find golden nuggets to expand where you already have the knowledge, to challenge the "that's how we've always done it" mindset, and to strive into new realms as you try something new.

If these critical Marketing areas inspire you but also leave you thirsting for more (or in need of help to get it accomplished!), then we encourage you to reach out to our thought leaders for additional help, coaching or consulting.

We believe this book will provide innovative ideas to drive your marketing efforts forward in a positive and effective way. Don't be afraid to think differently – that's how progress is made. So think outside the box and try new things. Join us on a journey as we explore how a little Marketing Fusion can impact your business in new and exciting ways.

~ Melanie Booher, INM President

1.

Marketing Strategy Blueprint

Kendra Ramirez, Kendra Ramirez Digital Agency

Your marketing strategy is the foundation of your marketing success. The mistake we see time and again is when we receive calls from potential clients and they are asking about a specific tool like building Facebook ads, SEO, content plan, or a LinkedIn company page. When we need to start with the actual strategy and business goals tied to that strategy before talking about tactics and tools. Let's talk through what your marketing strategy blueprint for your business success looks like.

The framework we use is:

1. Understand your audience
2. Conduct digital assessment
3. Define success
4. Create content
5. Measure
6. Optimize and repeat

Before diving into the framework, let's address your marketing mindset.

- **Mindset #1: Fear of doing it wrong.**
    - Your marketing strategy will always evolve. It is a living breathing thing just like your business plan. Marketing is about testing and learning. So, let go of those perfectionism traps. "Done" is better than perfect. We sometimes can become paralyzed with all the options in marketing. Just get started somewhere.
- **Mindset #: Fear of what to say.**
    - "How can I create content when everything I want to say has already been said?" Ok, let's use the example of Easter. What if every Pastor, Preacher, Priest or Minister said, "Well, the Easter story has already been told, so I don't need to tell it." ? The same principle applies here. People want your version of the topic. You are an influencer. People will respond and lean in to listen to what you have to say. The world has been around for thousands of years. So, in reality, there are no truly original thoughts.
- **Mindset #3: Fear of being seen.**
    - No one likes themselves on video or the sound of your voice. You sound and look amazing. Show up. We need you in this world. We need to see your face light up when you are talking about your passions. Visibility and vulnerability is what is winning in today's world.

- **Mindset #4- Fear of looking silly.**
    - Have you seen all the Reels on Instagram or videos on Tiktok? Lots of silly things are going on there. People like real and authentic content. We want to know you are human and not overly scripted. Don't worry about the "ums" and stumbling over and through your words. I am a big fan of one-take social videos. If you stumble, just keep going. Just keep swimming.
- **Mindset #5- Fear of doing it alone.**
    - Yes, someone needs to quarterback your marketing. Get your teams involved; or if you don't have a team, get your partners and clients involved. Hire a contractor or part-time employee to assist with execution when you are just getting started with your marketing efforts. You don't have to do it alone. The best marketing isn't done in a silo.

Now that we got rid of the "marketing scaries" let's dive into your marketing framework.

Your Target Audience

Understanding your target audience and what motivates them is another important step in the process. Most of the time, *you* are not your target audience. Don't guess what your audience needs from you. Let's start with, who do you serve? What problems do you solve? What challenges do your clients face? Diving deeper than just simply demographics of "male" or "female" or age range.

We love using the hero journey method that Don Miller provides at StoryBrand. The StoryBrand template will help you tell the story of **how** you guide your clients to success. Our clients love using this template. **You** are not the hero. Your **client** is the hero. You are the guide that helps get them to where they are going. This really flips the script when reviewing your home page or the "About Us" section on your website. People buy from people that they know, like, and trust.

Understand where your target audience plays and how they like to consume content. Everyone's learning style is different. You need to appeal to a variety of styles.

- Do they like to read?
- Do they like to watch videos?
- Do they like to listen to podcasts?
- Do they prefer an e-newsletter from you or do they prefer to follow you on social media?
- Which channels do they play on?
- Do they play on Facebook with older demographics?
- Or do they play on Instagram with younger demographics?
- Do they play on LinkedIn because they are more business to business oriented?

Who else also targets your audience in a noncompetitive way? Look for co-marketing opportunities with partners. Can you be a guest on each other's blog or podcast? Can you identify micro-influencers to work with as well? Do you have an opportunity to build a community with your audience?

Some examples of building community are as follows: a financial planning organization that hosts weekly "Coffee and Connect" sessions online. They rotate experts on each session that are there to serve their clients. No pitches, just holding space for connection and community. Another organization hosts monthly leader meetings to build peer-to-peer relationships and problem-solve together. Notice that both groups are there to serve others and bring knowledge to the table versus selling tactics.

If you are still struggling to understand your target audience don't be afraid to ask them directly or use HubSpot's free buyer persona template to help build out your target audience even more. Now that we better understand our target audience, let's create a content plan for them.

Digital Assessment

A digital assessment is a great baseline to help identify your marketing gaps. Start your digital assessment by looking at your website. Does your website speak directly to your target audience? Are they represented on your website? Are you talking to their challenges and how you can come alongside them and guide them through solving their challenges? Do you have a lead magnet on your website that someone could download or learn from where they would be willing to give you their email address to gain that knowledge from you? Do you have a "sign-up" for your e-newsletter? Do you have social integration? Do you have photos and videos representing your organization to tell your story? Is everything mobile-friendly? What social channels do you currently have? Is there brand consistency from the website to your proposal, to your social media channels?

Not only do you want to look at your own marketing, but you want to look at your competitors' marketing strategies as well. What services are they leading with on their website? How are they describing what they do? What social channels are they playing in? How often are they posting on those channels? What is your differentiation in the market? Why do people buy from you?

You can also look at a mentor brand. Finding a brand that you aspire to be like we find is often very helpful. Do you have a mission, vision, and values defined in your organization? How are you walking those out in your business and through your marketing today? Now that we have identified our marketing gaps, let's define our success.

Define Success

Start with the end in mind. We need to understand your business strategy. What are your business goals? What are you hoping to achieve through marketing, is it business development, recruitment, brand awareness, or customer service? Gaining clarity about your business goals will help drive your marketing goals and what success, for you, looks like. What's the most profitable thing that the organization does today? Is that particular service on your website? Define what marketing success looks like for your organization.

- Would you want more leads?
- More candidates?

- Increased brand awareness?
- More conversations?
- Or are you thinking of more leads, candidates, brand awareness, conversations?

Then ask yourself, "How is this success going to be measured?" Keep in mind it is easy to fall into the trap of vanity metrics: likes follows, or impressions. The good news is that it can be measured. This is a big myth that we hear often. Now that we know what success will look like for our marketing, let's dive into understanding the target audience that we serve.

Create Content

Now for the fun part: content creation. Ideas for content are everywhere. Look at your presentations, RFPs, proposals, recorded webinars that you have led or participated in, industry, and association content. Determine the frequency of posting content that you will be sharing. You don't have to post every day and on every platform. Take a phased approach. Our approach is the crawl, walk, and run method.

- What types of content are you going to post?
- Who's going to own the writing process of content?
- Who will add the visual elements to that content?

Ask yourself what are some of the "frequently asked questions" that we get from clients and candidates. This type of content is gold. Get your employees involved in the process. Empower your employees to share their ideas and content. Getting into a cadence for your monthly content plan is so critical to keep things moving in the right direction. We recommend doing batch content over a 30 day period. That way you're only having to touch it once a month or so; approve it and then everything gets scheduled out from there.

That's great but where do you go when you get stuck with coming up with content ideas? You can find more content ideas on Answer The Public, AllTop, Slideshare, Buzzsumo, YouTube, Twitter, Industry websites, Association websites, and from interviewing your clients and employees. Start an internal marketing committee and hold monthly content idea sessions with them. We like to call them "bad marketing ideas" meetings. This takes the pressure off of you and is a way more fun and engaging way to brainstorm and connect with your clients and employees.

When planning out content, ask yourself if there is anything coming up in the next 30-60-90 days that you need to include in your content plan. Don't shy away from video in your content plan. Your brain processes video 60,000 times faster than text. We get to actually see your passion on video versus you just writing about it. The videos don't have to be studio-quality videos for social media. There is nothing wrong with using your phone for quick videos. Now that we have a content plan, it's time to measure.

Measure

See the fruits of your labor. Pull your weekly or monthly reports from your website, social media channels, and e-newsletter. What are the numbers telling you?

For business development: Did we drive more traffic to our landing page? How many people downloaded your lead magnet? How many of those that downloaded it turned into a call? How many of those calls turned into proposals? How many proposals turned into clients? Know your close ratio.

For recruiting: Did we have more people on our careers page? How many filled out your application? How many interviews? How many offers were made? How many were onboarded? Know your days to fill ratio.

For customer service: Did the number of calls go down? Were you able to resolve the issue quicker?

For brand awareness: How many impressions and how much engagement did you have? How many people shared your content? What was your open rate on your emails? How many new subscribers did you get? How many unsubscribed?

You can use a simple spreadsheet to document your numbers from one month to the next month to look for trends. Document if your numbers are growing, decreasing or if they're flat. Then look for reasons as to why the numbers are changing. Did you have less content than the month before? Causing the numbers to fall from the previous month? Did you have a media opportunity or event that drove the numbers up? Now that we know what to measure and how let's optimize our process.

Optimize and Repeat

Optimizing your marketing starts with reviewing the last 30 days. Ask yourself, "What worked?" "What didn't work?" What types of content have resonated with your clients or candidates and what missed the mark? What channels were more successful than others?

Go back through the customer and candidate journey. Are there areas that can be tweaked or tightened up for a better close ratio?

Now that you have a marketing strategy blueprint to leverage, another important factor to remember in marketing is that consistency will pay off. You will have to pivot your plan as your audience and marketing platforms change. Remember that your marketing plan is an ever-evolving plan. Test, test, and test. Stay curious but don't get caught up in shiny objects without testing them before diving in. Be patient with yourself as marketing can be overwhelming. Just 10 years ago we only had 150 marketing tools, and today we have over 9,000 tools in our toolbox; new ones are being added daily.

We are often asked about the tools we use to execute for clients. Here is a shortlist of the essential tools that are often recommended:

Social Media Management Platform: Buffer, Agorapulse or Hootsuite

Design Tools: Canva, Ripl or Adobe Spark

Stock Photos and Images: Pexels, Canva, Unsplash or PicMonkey

Website Platforms: Wix, Squarespace or WordPress

SEO Tools: Yoast for WordPress and Moz.

Website Analytics: Google Analytics

E-Newsletter Platforms: MailChimp, Constant Contact, or Emma

Video Tools: iMovie, Animoto, Wave, and BigVu (for teleprompter on your phone)

Content Curation Tools: Tweetdeck, Feedly or Google alerts

Proofreading Tool: Grammarly

All the tools recommended are free or budget-friendly. You don't need all of them. Try a few of them and let us know how it is going for you. We look forward to hearing from you.

With a strong strategy in place, let's look at filling that pipeline using our six C's.

- Curious
- Connector
- Community
- Convert
- Care
- Consistent

Curious

Stay curious about your industry, your clients, your client's industry, and always be learning. Attend your client's industry conferences or webinars. Ask your clients to tell you more. Really lean in. I wouldn't be in the digital industry if I hadn't stayed curious. Digital didn't exist when I was in college. I love to learn and have the mentality of: "opportunities are around every corner." I fell in love with the digital industry. There will be other industries that pop up that don't exist today that you may find yourself falling in love with. In order to do that, you have to stay curious my friends.

Connector

Be a connector for others even when it isn't related to your specific job or company. An example is recently I saw a social media post about someone looking for additional commercial space for his growing photography business. I reached out to him and let him know about another friend who has beautiful commercial space and has space that he isn't using. It would be a "win, win" for them. This has nothing to do with my specific business but I enjoy connecting two wonderful people with great businesses. Be a connector for yourself, your team, and your clients. We all know business development is about timing. Timing is everything! Who do you think they will think of when you have assisted them in other areas of their business? You!

Community

Build a community or get involved in an existing community. This one is so vital, and something I am really passionate about. I have a friend who is a financial planner, and he started a Coffee and Connect community that meets online every Thursday. He brings in different speakers on different topics that the community would like to learn more about. Not once does he sell his services. It is about building a community and it has grown beyond his wildest dreams and beyond his local community. He has a thriving high six-figure business and he accompanies that directly tied to his community building. You can also get involved in existing communities that you have similar interests in like hiking, bike riding, crafting, and/or whatever else you might enjoy doing.

Convert

Converting is about having a lead magnet on your website. It's not enough to point someone to your website or a blog. Do you have a lead magnet on your website? Something that someone can provide an email address to receive the lead magnet. This can be a paid or free lead magnet. Examples of a lead magnet are downloadables like templates or checklists, reports, or invites to specific programs. This is an opportunity for someone to get a taste of what you offer or purchase your programs/services. These have always worked well for our clients. One client with a simple lead magnet for a plan that he was offering and they sold three new clients at $20,000 each. This was all done through organic traffic; not paid advertising. When you are speaking directly to your target audience and the solutions to their challenges this can be very effective.

Care

Care about your team, employees, clients, partners, and the community that you serve.

Surprise and delight them all. Make notes of when you hear about someone purchasing a new home, having a baby, getting married, birthdays, and work anniversaries. Celebrate it all. I surprised my team with some aromatherapy shower fizzes. A small surprise to thank them for their work and a way to treat themselves. We love surprising our clients around Thanksgiving with gifts of appreciation.

Caring will help prospective clients and candidates and retain current clients and team members. Ask yourself, how you can surprise and delight the people that you are surrounded by.

Consistent

Marketing must be consistent. You can't start and stop and expect to see results. There is nothing wrong with testing, but allow your campaign and plans to be tested for a while before changing directions too quickly. Again, think of the crawl, walk, run method. You don't have to do everything on day one. We believe in a phased approach. Find a cadence that works for you. If you plan on posting on social media platforms twice a week, then stick to the same days during that week. As humans we love routine and we get used to expecting your content or e-newsletter on those days. Don't give up. You never know who is reading your content. Many times, I have people tell me in person that they love our content but I never see them liking or commenting on our content. Remember you are planting seeds.

Which of the six C's are you going to try? Let us know.

Now you know our secrets to marketing success! Our clients that are using these marketing strategies have led to successful growth in their business development and recruitment generation. We can't wait to celebrate your success with you.

We have a 45-page marketing strategy workbook just for you that goes into more detail. The workbook can be downloaded at https://Kendraramirez.com/marketingworkbook.

Kendra Ramirez

Kendra Ramirez is the Founder and CEO of Kendra Ramirez Digital Agency.

She is globally recognized on the home page of LinkedIn.com, Women of Influence Award Winner, John Barrett Entrepreneur Vision Award recipient, Cincy Chic Woman of the Year, AMA Marketing Legend and a finalist for the Social Media Innovator of the Year. Since 2005, she has helped hundreds of organizations, including Fortune 500 companies, leverage digital technologies. Kendra has spent more than 15 years in technology companies as a change agent in sales, marketing and recruiting leadership for B2B customers.

Connect with Kendra:

https://www.kendraramirez.com/

https://www.linkedin.com/in/kendraramirez/

2.

The Touchy-Feely Truth About Marketing

Why Soft Skills are Critical in Storytelling

Katy Crossen, Threshold Marketing & Communications

Whoever said that soft skills aren't important has never met my puppy.

Johnny has an incredible amount of EQ, or emotional quotient, which is another way of saying emotional intelligence. Johnny the Mini Goldendoodle is touchy-feely to a T. His sensitivity is remarkable! And the more amazing thing is – he excels at these soft skills without even knowing it.

EQ is the ability to use your own emotions to dial into another person's mood. When you tap into your EQ skills, you can read the room to deliver the right message. By relying on your instincts to empathize, you can help defuse a situation or overcome a challenge. You can use your inherent "spidey senses" to figure out what a person is feeling and respond appropriately.

Johnny has this skill in spades. He knows when I've spent too much time staring at my computer and will bark incessantly until I engage in a five-minute game of fetch. When I have worn myself out, Johnny is immediately worn out, too. He forces me to take a breath, hit pause, and rest; all by scurrying under the couch to take a nap, his legs splayed out like a little pork roast.

He can also tell when I'm excited. He can tell when I'm tired. Johnny can tell when I feel defeated and need some puppy cuddles before I can carry on. This little, blond furball is my ride-or-die. I can only hope my clients would say the same about me.

Soft skills – that intuitive ability to read people – transcend beyond the love of man's best friend. The ability to read the room (literally or figuratively), be sensitive, and then respond with an appropriate message is the foundation for a successful marketing strategy and its supporting messaging. That's the heart of a good story, and to me, that's what marketing is all about.

The goal is to tell a story that connects and resonates with your prospect and helps them develop an emotional connection that compels a reaction.

In this chapter, we're going to dig into the inner workings of marketing – how data alone can't sell a service or product. A story does. We'll also highlight a few ways to put this ideology into action.

What's the Story, Morning Glory?

My relationship with emotional storytelling started at an early age. Mrs. Sadler was my 2nd-grade teacher at Maple Dale Elementary, a spirited public school north of Cincinnati, Ohio. Mrs. Sadler was a woman in her early 60s. She loved turquoise jewelry and her face was well worn with smile lines and crinkles in the corners of her eyes that immediately let you know she'd led a good and happy life. She drove a big Cadillac and I thought she was the absolute coolest. Mrs. Sadler was also crazy about poetry. She taught her class of energetic if rambunctious, 7 and 8-year-olds about the magic of couplets and rhyming words. Stanzas and similes. Haikus and harmony.

I loved **all** of it. I loved the play with words. I loved the idea of *sta. ca. to.* sounds. If there was such a thing as a Second Grade Poetry Slam, I would have made my mom drive me there in her pea-green Honda Accord. Snaps and all.

Mrs. Sadler taught me that I could have fun with words; And that the words I said, the words I wrote, could compel someone to laugh or feel wistful. That with a turn of a phrase, it was the next best thing to inviting someone to step inside my skin and feel my feelings.

A year later, my interest in writing poems transitioned to an insatiable appetite for journalism. On a cold, January morning, our entire 3rd Grade class piled into a classroom, sitting on the carpet criss-cross applesauce, to watch a teacher go to space with a crew of astronauts. We were so little. Eyes wide open and curious about what was going to happen. And then we grew even more curious. Should we clap? Should we cheer? What's that big, orange cloud?

"Is this what's supposed to happen?" we asked.

That night, my mom held my little sister in a rocking chair as we watched Tom Brokaw deliver the nightly news. The newscast was wall-to-wall with coverage about the Challenger explosion. It was a pivotal moment for a teary, blue-eyed girl who had a lot of questions that all started with, "Why?"

From that point on, I sat at the kitchen table every morning and clipped articles about the Challenger out of The Cincinnati Enquirer. I saved each one in a manila folder my dad gave me; I was obsessed with knowing more. O-rings. Extra cold temperatures at launch time. Profiles on each of the seven crew members. The stories were crushing and a lot for a 9-year-old to absorb, but they instantly created a connection that tethered me to a new passion: knowing and reporting the news.

Fast forward 10 years and I was pursuing a degree in journalism at the University of Kentucky. It was the mid to late 90s and we were listening to Oasis and wearing platform shoes. Part of my course work brought me back to my passion of poetry, but the writer in me knew working as a journalist would be a more viable path for earning a living. I spent two years writing for The Kentucky Kernel, the school newspaper, and my favorite assignment was writing a regular column during my last semester.

As a columnist, I had to dig deep into the things I was feeling, the things I observed as a senior in college. Writing a column comes with an unwritten understanding that you'll be a little vulnerable. You'll take some risks by taking sides. Those pieces were my favorite to write because they involved sharing my stories with transparency. Those pieces were the ones that my professors and classmates commented on most. In the months leading up to graduation, I started developing a following, and other columnists began responding to my original pieces with columns of their own. I may have been in journalism school, but I solved an equation that I never forgot.

Empathy + Convincing Storytelling = Emotional Connection

And to take that a step further:

Convincing Storytelling + Emotional Connection = Desired Reaction

After college, I spent 10 years working as a newscast producer, and emotional stories were still my favorite pieces to write and produce.

Who Wrote the Book of Love?

As a former journalist, I firmly believe that data substantiates a story. Now that I'm a consultant, I regularly collaborate with clients who want to make bold claims in their marketing and communications about their business model, revenue successes, or unique product or service. I typically ask the client to tell me more. *What data points do you have? How can we substantiate this position?* Sometimes that line of questioning compels the team to hit pause and really think about what claims they can truly own.

Metrics and facts are a framework that is undeniable. You can make the claims if you have the receipts to back them up. There's another critical element to telling a story or launching a marketing initiative. I call it the magic of marketing – that ephemeral, emotional messaging that hooks someone in and has them hanging on your every word. That enchanting messaging is what helps a brand create connections with prospects and bonds partners together.

Several years ago, I was working in-house for a dynamite B2B firm, and the business development team was led by an executive who exudes charm. He telegraphed a sincere passion for his colleagues and customers, and I learned a tremendous amount by studying what this sales executive cared about, and how he expressed it. It was at this stage in my professional career that I analogized that sales and marketing are a lot like dating; dating leans heavily into EQ traits.

It turns out, maintaining a repeat customer is a lot like maintaining a relationship with a romantic prospect. Yes, sometimes you send gifts or plan special outings over cocktails. The real bonding happens when you can prove you're listening to your prospect. You share stories that convey a clear understanding of their challenges, their goals, and their weaknesses. Your message is undeniable and unwavering: *I hear you. I know you. I want to be your partner.*

In a B2B world, it's easy for some firms to lose sight of this simple act of wooing. EQ skills are often written off as soft skills, and some B2B firms prize analytical skills and technical prowess over the sensitivity and intuition required to maintain client relationships. Think back to your dating history and the relationships that were successful versus the ones that failed.

I've dated partners who were great when it came to changing a tire and other partners who excelled at creating spreadsheets that broke down vacation budgets by line item. As time passed by, I learned how to change my own tires and create my own vacation matrixes. It turns out, my favorite partners were people who invested in getting to know me better; people who had excellent communication skills and knew just what to say when I was trying to overcome a challenge or pursue a new goal.

The best partners leaned into their listening and empathy and sincerely said the right things. It was endearing, and our relationships lasted longer than those that involved poor communicators.

Read that line again, but this time, think about it in the context of marketing.

The best partners leaned into their listening and empathy and sincerely said the right things. It was endearing, and our relationships lasted longer than those that involved poor communicators.

That's basically a two-sentence primer about successful marketing. Listen, empathize, deploy messaging that grows connections. Repeat.

Love Will Keep Us Together

Okay, Katy. We get it. You really like telling stories and being vulnerable and empathetic. But why should we believe you?

I hear you. It's true. I'm not an expert on industrial psychology. For that, I refer you to the writings of Simon Sinek and Adam Grant; the latter of whom has been fundamental in my professional growth (I especially recommend Grant's book, Give and Take). If you buy into that whole, "It takes 10,000 hours of practice to become an expert" ideology, then I am an expert in storytelling.

With nearly 25 years of professional writing under my belt, I've logged a lot of copy. Copy that has been read over the airwaves by dozens of TV anchors. Hundreds of deeply personal (and sometimes embarrassing) blog posts that I began chronicling at the start of the "new" millennium. Pages and pages of marketing content for industries ranging from commercial real estate to quick-service restaurants.

In newsrooms and boardrooms, I've had the chance to see which stories resonate best with their intended audience. In some instances, my storytelling sold an idea or a product, and other times my messaging sold me or my employer. I believe I am most successful as a writer when I craft copy from a place of inspiration; my goal every time is to tap into my emotions to help that inspiration transcend from the words on the page to galvanize and energize the reader. I firmly believe that the best marketing messaging comes from a place of sincere emotion.

I'm not alone in this feeling.

Research shows that empathy is the most important leadership trait. A recent article in Forbes says that empathy is not a soft skill, but a critical trait that supports the bottom line. The article cited a study at Georgetown University that found that incivility in the workplace can create diminished performance, inhibit collaboration, and damage the customer experience.[1]

I don't have to think too hard to remember occasions in which I've been in a brusque environment – both in the workplace and on the receiving end as the customer.

In the former scenario, I've toughed it out and kept my head down because I needed the paycheck. As a customer, I've canceled vendor contracts and walked out of restaurants. It's easy to cut bait on a relationship when you don't feel appreciated, understood, or respected.

Just as we can demonstrate empathy to maintain relationships with our colleagues, we can rely on those same sensitivity skills to initiate and grow relationships with our customers. It's important to channel your EQ strengths and talk with target constituents about their pain points and the challenges they're trying to overcome. It sounds a bit *cliched*, but that old chestnut of, "What keeps you up at night?" is an important question to ask. Once we're armed with those worries, we can develop messaging that creates awareness, educates, and finally convince our prospects as they consider their purchase decision.

Said another way, empathy is a critical part of the marketing funnel because it helps us nurture our target audience and get them to yes.

First date -> Engagement Proposal -> Marriage. Sales and marketing are like dating.

Can't Stop the Feeling!

There's another big factor to consider as we talk about EQ and marketing. Every marketer needs to acknowledge that there are generational differences at play in the workplace. The message you deploy may need a little finesse depending on the decision-maker receiving your content. Depending on which source you read, Millennials are either the **MOST** empathetic or **LEAST** empathetic generation in the workplace. Let's dig into this a little bit, shall we?

A 2018 article from Forbes reported that Millennials are the most empathetic and mature generation yet.[2] Five years prior, Time Magazine called Millennials the "Me Me Me Generation," complete with a cover photo of a young woman taking a selfie and a subtitle that claimed Millennials were lazy, entitled narcissists who still live with their parents.[3] Still another article, this time in 2015 by HR Magazine, reported that Millennials have higher emotional intelligence than previous generations in the workplace.[4]

Whiplash, anyone?

Perhaps the jury is still out on Millennials and their younger cohort, Generation Z. There has been plenty of information reported that indicates the youngest generations in the workplace are committed to altruistic values. Millennials represent significant philanthropic beliefs and make personal and professional purchasing decisions based on whether a business reflects their shared values.

It's a bridge too far to say that a for-profit business can position itself in the same philanthropic light the way a non-profit organization can, but it's fair to make a connection between altruism and the storytelling techniques we demonstrate to engender our services and products with the younger generations. Remember those spidey senses mentioned at the start of this chapter? Millennials give us a critical opportunity to lean into those EQ skills as we craft content to nurture them through the marketing funnel.

In some instances, and depending on the prominence of the millennial, a marketer may need to tailor their message to consider younger customers who can influence major B2B purchasing decisions.

This idea takes Account-Based Marketing to a hyper-focused level that isn't realistic to execute on a macro level: there's no way you could devise a custom marketing program for every Millennial who ever considered buying an iPhone. If a Millennial is a primary decision-maker for a family office considering a major investment, it's completely worth leaning into your soft skills and determining what marketing strategy and the message would best resonate with your princely prospect.

Honestly, you'd want to craft a custom marketing program for a family office decision-maker, regardless of whether they were a Millennial or not. The story you tell would need to heavily rely on your soft skills; your intuition and empathy for your prospect and what messaging would best resonate based on their pain points, challenges, and opportunities. Then, you'll want to build an entire marketing campaign with extremely focused messaging – targeted content and experiential – to communicate with the prospect.

I once worked for an advertising agency that bought outdoor billboards at strategic locations to directly target a single, influential decision-maker. Our media buyer pinpointed billboards that the prospect would pass on their morning commute from their home to the office. The team would feign surprise when the executive mentioned that they saw the billboards and thought the billboards were a brilliant coincidence. "You don't say!" we would giggle. In today's digital and mobile age, I might instead choose very targeted mobile geofencing.

If you want to catch a fish, fish where the fish are.

End of the Road

I've covered how EQ is an inherent trait in each of us. We're each hard-wired to be empathetic and can use those skills to respond in a genuine way to compel a reaction in a person. Some of us can flex those empathy muscles better than others, but with a little practice, each of us can easily get in touch with our inner sensitivity.

This chapter also highlighted my take on what makes the best storytelling: inspired messaging that creates a palpable sense of emotion that transcends the written word and helps the reader closely identify with the writer's spirit and intent.

I also delved into how storytelling takes a message beyond facts and data and uses a lot of the same sincerity found in dating relationships, with a similar goal of getting our prospect to say: *yes*. I also took a closer look at why empathy is one of the most important traits for leadership, and that marketers need to lean into EQ when they consider storytelling and content for the many generations in the workplace.

Johnny the Mini Goldendoodle, dating, the Challenger explosion, and subtle, section-by-section music references. This chapter has been vulnerable; sharing stories that you have hopefully found to be endearing and empathetic.

The final parting nugget I must share is less of a pearl of wisdom and more of a grain of platitude. *Everything is a good time or a good story.* Lean into the good times and good stories you've gathered throughout life. When you're working on messaging, reflect on the things you know and the things you've experienced. Use those planks to build a bridge that helps you connect with your audience.

The best stories we can tell are those that are full of memories and experiences we can enthusiastically claim as our own.

Notes

1. Tracy Brower, Forbes.com, 9/19/2021, https://www.forbes.com/sites/tracybrower/2021/09/19/empathy-is-the-most-important-leadership-skill-according-to-research/?sh=67402fe73dc5
2. Sarah Landrum, Forbes.com, 1/19/2018, https://www.forbes.com/sites/

sarahlandrum/2018/01/19/millennials-are-happiest-when-they-feel-connected-to-their-co-workers/?sh=1bc5bf3a3a2f

3. Joel Stein, Time.com, 5/20/2013, https://time.com/247/millennials-the-me-me-me-generation/
4. Becky Frith, HR Magazine, 10/9/2015, https://www.hrmagazine.co.uk/content/other/millennials-have-higher-emotional-intelligence

Katy Crossen

Katy Crossen has nearly 25 years of marketing and communications experience including several leadership-level strategy roles, but she got her start honing the craft of storytelling in the belly of a newsroom.

Prior to founding Threshold Marketing & Communications, Crossen served as an account director at a global B2B advertising agency. Here, she led teams serving Fortune 500 clients including Target Corporation, Canon, and Viacom. Katy fell in love with B2B marketing and communications during the five years she oversaw marketing and communications strategy for a multi-market, commercial real estate developer and construction firm based in Cincinnati.

Crossen's career began in broadcasting, in which she spent 10 years producing newscasts for the CBS and ABC affiliates in Cincinnati, OH and Lexington, KY, respectively. Her philosophy on marketing and communications comes straight from those days of working in

TV news: with a focus on the people you want to target, the message you want to communicate, and the channels you're using to reach them.

When she isn't growing her business or helping clients grow theirs, Katy is plotting a far-flung travel adventure or savoring a delicious glass of Kentucky bourbon at her home in Downtown Cincinnati.

Connect with Katy:

https://www.thresholdmarcom.com/

https://www.linkedin.com/in/katycrossen/

3.

Build Your Brand of Brilliance

Peg Stookey, MaxPotential U

Introduction:

As I began writing this chapter, I knew that business leaders would be reading Marketing Fusion. Since marketing is not just the owner's job, it's also possible that others will be looking for guidance and insight on marketing. I firmly believe that each individual is the CEO of themselves and their careers, families, etc. And just as they are the CEO, they are the CMO or Chief Marketing Officer. So, although I primarily address business leaders, please know that this chapter is for you, regardless of your title.

With that, let's begin!

Personal Brand: Why Should You Care and Why Now?

Whether you're the business owner, an expert building a reputation, or a customer-facing employee, your brand matters. Potential customers are searching for you before you even meet them. I was shocked when a referral told me that he'd read everything I'd ever written on LinkedIn. My first thought was to go back through my articles and posts and do some editing!

My second thought was to learn more. First, I thanked the gentleman for his interest, and then I asked him for his overall impression. What had he learned about me? As he detailed his thoughts, I realized that he felt like he KNEW me, liked me, and could TRUST me. Know, like, and trust: the goal of any marketer!

The point is that people are finding you, they will see you or read about you, and they will judge you AND your organization. You will leave an impression, and that impression is an essential element of your brand.

It's also an element that you can control! While you don't know if someone might land on your website "About" page or LinkedIn profile at 3:30 AM on a sleepless night, you can ensure that what they see and learn is of your choosing.

The opposite is true. Not caring, or being lazy about it, can cause irreparable harm. Your sales process starts with marketing, and your marketing begins with YOU. You're the center of the marketing ripple that reaches out to your potential customers.

What is a Personal Brand?

It's highly likely that you're associated with an organizational brand

and indeed that you're aware of product or service brands. Look around you. Can you spot a product that represents a brand? My husband's iWatch is on the desk, close to where I'm typing. iWatch is an example of a BIG brand, Apple, and a sub-brand, iWatch, and even the entire line of i-Somethings like iPad, iPod, etc. What do you know about these brands? What is your impression? What judgments are you making based on what you know for sure AND what you think you might know (your assumptions)?

According to William Arruda, arguably the father of modern personal branding, your brand is your "Unique Promise of Value," which I refer to as your "Brand of Brilliance." However you define it, it's the shining beacon that calls attention to you. And whether you care or not, or you've worked on it or not, YOU HAVE A BRAND! That's the scariest truth you'll ever hear from me. Embrace it or not, you are a brand, and it reflects on all areas of your work and life!

Clarifying Your Brand Purpose

Your brand precedes and follows you. It's also something you can take control of with just a little motivation, which starts by defining your Brand Purpose.

To name your Brand Purpose, you need to create a sense of urgency and find the answer to *Why is my brand important NOW?*

Regardless of your particular reason, here's the WHY NOW that many are experiencing: **The Internet.** The Internet is a how-did-we-ever-live-without-it tool that can help you grow your business/career, but it can also be a force of destruction if you're not careful how you use it. Knowing and accepting this fact should create a sense of urgency all on its own.

To help determine the answer to Why Now, do an Internet search for your name and business. What do you find? What are the first four or five entries that pop up? Are they current? You might find an old bio and photo on a former employer's website, or maybe you learn that you have more than one LinkedIn profile. Hopefully, you won't find any nefarious information, but if you do, wouldn't it be good to know about it?

Name two or three reasons that working on your brand is important NOW:

| |
| |
| |

Summarize the above insights into a Brand Purpose Statement:

| |
| |
| |

Here's my current* Brand Purpose as an example:

My Personal Brand is important to me now because I'm determined to build my Personal Brand Strategy and Change Readiness Coaching business 100% through referrals. In the future, what my referral partners perceive as my brand is critical to their willingness to introduce me to future clients. The impression my potential clients have of me directly affects their motivation to engage with me.

*Based on your current circumstances and sense of urgency, your Brand Purpose may change over time.

My goal is to help you kickstart the Building of your Brand of Brilliance. Once you have insight into your Brand Purpose, you're ready to start inventorying your Brand ASSETS & VALUE.

Are you comfortable with the idea that you're brilliant? I hope so! The fact is that every one of us has a unique set of innate strengths, gifts, and talents. We study and learn different things, develop a sense of enjoyment from engaging in various activities, and our passions and purpose evolve uniquely for each of us.

What a glorious thing individuality is!

And yes, we all have our weaknesses and failings as well. To find your Brand of Brilliance, can we agree not to focus on the negative?

Look at marketing as the truth that serves you well. For example, Coca-Cola spends billions on marketing their soda as The Real Thing. In their ads, we see sweaty athletes quenching their thirst with a bottle of iced cold Coke. REALLY? Does drinking 12 ounces of a sugar-laden fizzy drink quench thirst? Not so much. Speaking of the 12 teaspoons of sugar in a can of Coke, while laws demand that bottlers disclose the ingredients, they don't tell you whether they're good or bad for you, nor does Coke volunteer this information in its marketing.

When marketing yourself and your brand, let's focus on the positive and minimize the negative, just as all iconic brands do! And please note, this is NOT lying! **It's simply telling the truth that serves you well.**

I'd like to propose a few questions/exercises to help you unearth your brilliance, aka, positive attributes.

1. **What are your primary STRENGTHS?** In addition to answering the question for yourself, I encourage you to take the Clifton StrengthsFinder 2.0® assessment, https://store.gallup.com/p/en-us/10108/top-5-cliftonstrengths. Order the version that reveals your Top 5 strength characteristics, not the one that lays out the total spectrum of 34 traits. Why? Our brains process information about strengths and weaknesses differently, putting significantly more emphasis on weaknesses. This processing is called Negativity Bias. You should avoid the use of Negativity Bias for this exercise. What are your Top 5 Strengths based on your feedback and/or that of StrengthsFinder?

2. **What do others say is good about you?** You may have this data already from a 360 assessment or testimonials. If not, send an email to a few people that you trust and ask, "What is good about me? I know that I have weaknesses, but for this exercise, I'm simply asking for your positive impressions!" Summarize your responses. How do they compare to your strength insights?

3. **What's Unique & Special about you?** Pretend that you and your "brand twin" are both waiting to be interviewed for a job. You're struck by how much this other person looks like you. You're the same age, general build, hair color, etc. Your "twin" goes to the restroom but leaves a resume on the chair next to you. You glance at it and are

shocked. Your "twin's" resume looks almost exactly like yours! Upon returning from the restroom, your "twin" is immediately called into the interview. Here's your chance! What can you come up with in 20 minutes to help you stand out?

The above self-reflection work is life-changing! It helps build your confidence, create ideas for your future, and raise awareness of your brand. Building your Brand of Brilliance is a step-by-step process. Now that you have some idea of what assets you have to work with, let's dive into BRAND Awareness!

Unleash Your Brand

As a coach, wife, parent, business partner, friend, and more, I've learned that almost every problem originates through poor communication. Let's not let your brand suffer and negatively affect your future due to poor communication.

Communication is at minimum a two-way exercise, whether it's in person, over the phone, or through digital means. Use of communication for numerous purposes such as informing, influencing, learning, praising, correcting, selling, raising awareness, and more. It comes in various forms, such as written, verbal, visual, auditory, and more!

Let's narrow our scope so that you can get something out of this exercise. Because the next section of this chapter will focus on using LinkedIn to build your brand, I'd like to use LinkedIn as our communication example but know that it is only one area where you communicate your brand. Many of the principles cross-pollinate, as you'll see.

To prepare for excellent communication on and through your LinkedIn profile, I have some questions for you to consider:

WHO is/are your desired audience(s)?

Why are they important to you, or what is your interest in impressing them?

Who and what matters most to them, especially as it concerns you?

For example, two closely related demographics of my audience are small business owners and experts (coaches, consultants, authors, speakers, etc.).

They are essential to me because, as a business owner and expert myself, I have a particular affinity for them and care deeply about their hard-earned success. Plus, they often struggle with what comes easy for me….telling the story of their brilliance!

Understanding what matters most to my audience is often complicated because family, work, community, etc., are so intertwined for the small business owner and expert. In general, though, their Personal Brand matters because it is so intimately tied to the success of their business brand. There's a lot of motivation for all of us to get it right!

Your ability to confidently communicate your brand will come with time and effort. Practice, Practice, Practice! Work on your 30-second introduction and your longer (but not too long!) answer to the query, "Tell me about yourself." Pay attention to brands that impress you. More than anything, take a little risk, be somewhat vulnerable, and always be your very brilliant self!

Considering your Brand Purpose, Strengths, Audience, Uniqueness, etc. take a stab at defining your Brand of Brilliance:

Along with my expertise in career change readiness, personal branding, and career storytelling, I've developed a love for LinkedIn and its endless ability to help professionals move forward and attract what they need and want. That passion has earned me an element of expertise as well, and now I'd like to share it with you.

Build Your Brand of Brilliance Using LinkedIn

You present your brand to the world in virtually everything you do: How you answer the phone, the voicemail message that a caller hears, your email signature, your bio on your website, how you introduce yourself, your resume that lives online and gets sent to potential employers, and, of course, your growing social media/online presence.

We're going to focus on one of these areas specifically because it's so prevalently used by professionals and because doing so is an excellent brand creation platform. Of course, I'm talking about LinkedIn!

This topic could be an entire book itself, and if you know anything about LinkedIn, as soon as the book was published, it would be obsolete. LinkedIn is constantly improving and making changes. My goal with this section is to share some current, as of late 2021, branding ideas that will also help you become more confident in your use of LinkedIn, now and into the future. Just know that some of the specific "how-to's" may have changed by the time you're reading this.

To this end, we're going to play a game of **LinkedIn Show & Tell** because LinkedIn gives us many opportunities to leverage both communication styles!

But first, you'll want to have your LinkedIn profile in editing mode. Why LinkedIn doesn't just say "edit," I'll never know! To get into editing mode from your browser, click on the Me tab at the top of the page and then on "View Profile."

From your mobile app, click on your picture at the top of the page and then click on "View Profile."

You're now in editing mode, and you know that for sure because you see little pencils like this:

Now, let's begin by finding areas of your LinkedIn profile that are ripe and ready to TELL your audience about you.

Headline.

Your Headline is the line of words found right under your photo at the top of your LinkedIn profile. LinkedIn believes this area is crucial for automatically creating a Headline from your most recent Title and Employer, e.g., Chorale Director at Westminster Abbey.

While that Headline is informative, it isn't beneficial to the director's brand. They would want to jazz it up, use more available characters, and highlight themselves more fully. Additionally, your Headline is highly searchable by recruiters, potential customers, etc., so thousands will potentially see it. Here are some Headline Tips:

- Maximum character count: 220
- Capitalize each of the main words but not words such as of, to, it, etc.
- You can write it in complete sentences, but it's more impactful if you summarize your thoughts into sections separated by a pipe character (|), found under the backspace key, on the forward-slash key. You can also insert a symbol that is meaningful to you, such as a star, as a separator.

- Judiciously use keywords in your Headline. (Keywords are those that your audience will input into a search to find you. They're not magic words, but they do require some thought to identify.)

Contact info

Go to your LinkedIn profile and open up your Contact Info. What are others seeing? Is it current? Is it complete? Here are a few thoughts and tips for completing your Contact Info:

- **LinkedIn URL**: Be sure to customize your URL as you'll want to add it to your resume, business cards, email signature, etc. You can edit your URL from the top right of your profile while you're in editing mode. HINT: remove the letters and numbers after your name but keep your name the same. You may have to try several iterations to find a unique URL:

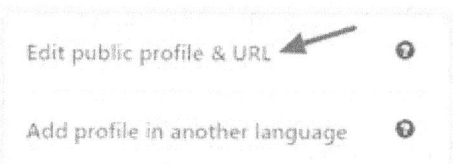

- **Website**: You can have up to three websites highlighted in your Contact Info. Depending on your situation, you might include: links to a company website, your bio on your company website, a scheduling service such as Calendly, social media site (like Facebook or Instagram), a personal marketing page, etc. Something to note: to the right of the URL you insert, there will be a dropdown. Click on "other"

and customize your description of the URL. So, instead of it saying "Company," you might change it to "XYZ Company Website" or "Schedule Time With Me!"

About Summary:

The About section is your primary opportunity to share your brilliance, so you need to strategize this section carefully. Here are some best practices to consider:

- Write it in FIRST person, using I, Me, We, etc. "Pretend" that your ideal audience member is reading your About summary. How would you speak to them?

- You have 2600 characters, including spaces and lines between paragraphs, which each count as a character. I always get asked if using all 2600 is too much. My response is that, of course, it's too much of what you write isn't interesting! On the flip side, 20 characters are too much if they're just dull words on the page. Be compelling!

- Open with an attention-grabbing paragraph to ensure that your reader clicks on "See More…" to open the rest of your summary.

- No matter how long it is, write in short paragraphs, two to four sentences at the most. This clear and concise writing is a general rule for digital copy. Human eyes and brains tend to get very antsy when reading online copy, and you don't want to lose your audience's attention.

- Tell a story or stories. Use examples to highlight the best of who you are and what you do.

- For business owners, it's often easier to talk about your business than yourself but, I encourage you to use this prime space to share some of who and why YOU are more authentically. Note: You'll have plenty of room in your Experience area to go into depth on what you do. Use your About to help people get to KNOW you!

- Close with a call to action. Think carefully. What do you want your visitor to do next? Should they connect with you, follow you, send you a referral, visit your Company Page or website, schedule an informational call, etc.?

Experiences:

If they put any content into their Experience descriptions, most people simply copy and paste their resume bullet points. Here's your chance to STAND OUT! If someone asked you to tell them about your career, how would you respond? Let's look at a few tips for leveraging this underutilized section of your LinkedIn profile:

- EACH Experience has a maximum of 2000 characters to tell your story of success in that role.

- Again, write your Experiences in the FIRST person.

- As you should in your resume, focus on accomplishments, not just your responsibilities or job description.

- Unlike your resume, write in complete sentences!

- Tip: Try writing your experiences from the bottom up or from the furthest away job to present, just as you would tell your career story to a real person.

- Continue reading to learn more about using the Experience section to SHOW your brilliance.

Accomplishments, Education, and additional background:

Filling in the blanks of your whole life and career can go a long way to helping you Build Your Brand of Brilliance. Before you document every volunteer opportunity or class you've taken, re-look at your Brand Purpose. Your LinkedIn profile should be shaping up as a strong representation of your Brand. Adding in a few thoughts on WHY you chose to go to the college you attended or volunteered in a particular role can help others get to know you in a positive light.

Skills:

Like most of LinkedIn, your Skills section is highly searchable. Completing your Skills can help recruiters and potential customers and employees find you. I train my clients to revisit their Skills yearly, at a minimum. This revisit ensures that their profiles are optimized and up to date. You can have a maximum of 50 skills. Be sure to highlight all 50, and don't forget the ever-important soft skills!

It's time to SHOW YOUR BRILLIANCE!

Except for your photo, which is mandatory, most of the suggestions in this Show section are additional elements or techniques that make your profile pop and move your brand from exciting and accurate to STAND OUT BRILLIANT!

Background Banner:

This background banner is the area behind your photo and is the first thing your profile visitor will see. It's also a brand opportunity that many miss! You can use the minimal backgrounds that LinkedIn provides, create your own, or engage someone with graphic design skills. I use Canva or Stencil to build them because I don't need graphic design skills, and those platforms offer formatting that fits LinkedIn's requirements.

- Use color! Do you have a favorite personal brand color?

- If you have a business, you could highlight its brand by imposing your logo and contact info onto the background. You might need a graphic designer and if you do hire one, be sure to get your LinkedIn Company Page banner done as well! Check out www.fiverr.com or other freelance sites for inexpensive designers!

- I love adding a meaningful quote or saying to an individual's banner or a catchy tagline for a company's banner. With a bit of added effort, a quote SHOWS so much about you and your brand! FYI-Stencil is my go-to resource for creating these kinds of banners. You can access my affiliate link here: https://getstencil.com/a/ref/accnaf8fafab.

Photo:

A current photo is a MUST! But it doesn't have to be a formal headshot taken by a professional photographer. Or, it can be! Just be sure that if someone were to look at your photo before meeting with you for the first time, they'd be able to recognize you. Several years ago, I was using a photo where I was not yet wearing glasses full-time. At one of our sessions, a client mentioned that my photo didn't look like me because I wasn't wearing glasses. Oh my! She was right! Here are a few additional photo tips:

- Before your photo shoot, look through several LinkedIn profile photos. What positively catches your eye?
- Avoid a cluttered background. I usually prefer a darker background.
- Remember that this is a professional platform, so don't use pictures that include your pets or kids unless that's an essential element of your brand.
- Wear darker clothing and avoid stripes, plaids, or very busy prints.
- When posting your photo, zoom in through the LinkedIn Zoom feature to make your head very visible.
- Because we're using LinkedIn to build relationships and make fantastic impressions, consider positioning yourself so that it will appear that you're looking right at your profile visitor. To do so, turn your head slightly to the left and look forward toward the camera. So simple, but it works!

Featured Section:

The "featured section" is a relatively new area of LinkedIn and is ideal to SHOW your brand! Like all of the optional profile sections, Featured will show up once you add content to it. If you don't have it yet, go to my profile to see an example: www.linkedin.com/in/

pegstookey. Scroll to below the About section. You'll notice that the Featured area is highly visual, which is why we're using it to SHOW your Brilliance! One of the primary benefits of this area is that, unlike older posts that get hidden in your Activity area, whatever you post as Featured will stay there until you change it. Keep this in mind as you attach new elements and move them around. Keep it fresh and Brand Relevant! In this section, you can

- Attach a LinkedIn post or article by making it Featured (once posted, click on the three dots in the post's upper right corner and then click on Make it Featured).
- By clicking the plus sign in the Featured section, you can also attach videos, pictures, pdfs, and more!

Fancy Text and Symbols:

As you probably realize, LinkedIn doesn't allow any formatting such as Bold, Italics, different fonts, etc. on any of your profile copy. But you may have seen profiles that use symbols, bold, italics, etc., and wonder how they do it. The answer is "fancy text!" Fancy text generators take your text copy and convert it to various symbols that look like formatted text. The generator that I use is https://www.thefancytext.com/.

Related is that you can't automatically generate bullet points throughout your LinkedIn profile, yet bullets are a great way to itemize your thoughts and create interest. To get around LinkedIn's constraints, you can

- Use a dash (-) or less than (>) character to denote a bullet.

- Use a symbol to represent a bullet point. To do so, use a source for symbols such as Emojipedia (https://emojipedia.org/). Copy the symbol and paste it into your LinkedIn copy. Note that if you want to indent your "bullets," you'll have to add spaces and sometimes the spaces don't stay lined up. I don't usually bother with the indentation.
- Note: You can also use symbols to separate sections in your Headline.

Using fancy text and symbols can significantly enhance the show-ability of your profile, but too much can be more damaging than not using them at all. As you choose to add in visual elements, stay true to your brand and ensure that your visuals enhance, not detract from your message!

Properly connected Experiences/Accomplishments:

One of the fastest, most effective ways to add visual interest to your profile is to properly connect your Experiences (and Education and Organizations) to their associated Company Pages. FYI-LinkedIn has shortened this phrase to "Page," but I find it confusing, so I'll stick to Company Page for clarity.

The important message is that by connecting the Company Page to the Experience, you'll ensure that the Company's logo shows up instead of a generic logo box; AND your visitor won't be sent to a general search page.

A generic logo might also mean that the Company didn't attach a logo to their Company Page, or they might not have a Company Page. In either case, you might not be able to do anything about it unless you're the owner and decide to put up a Company Page (see below for instructions).

To correctly attach your Company's Page to your Experience:

- Scroll down your profile and look for any generic logo boxes like this:
- While in editing mode, open the Experience by clicking on the "pencil" to the right side of the Experience box.
- If you already have an Experience section for your current Company but not a logo, put your cursor on the line for the Company. If there's a Company Page available, you should see a popup below the line with the company name and logo.
- If you're creating a new Experience, start typing your company name into the appropriate line. As long as there's a Company Page for the organization, you'll see a popup for it.
- CLICK ON THE POPUP. This step is crucial and is how you correctly connect your Experience to the Company Page. If you don't see the popup, highlight the Company's name to see if it shows up. If none of that works, it probably means that there isn't a Company Page. You can double-check this by typing the name of the Company into your Search bar.

Aside from adding visual interest with the logos, properly connecting your Experiences, etc., is vital in helping your visitors learn more about you and your career history. With a simple click in your Experience box, this will take visitors to the Company Page. They can learn more about what your organization does and will have the opportunity to Follow your Page and go directly to your website.

Special NOTE for business owners, experts, and organizational leaders:

Regardless of the size of your organization, you should put up a Company Page. It's imperative that your profile visitors can quickly go from your profile to your Company Page. If you don't have one, or it's not correctly connected, the company page will take them to a general search page which might not serve you well, especially if that page brings up your competitors and not your Company.

How to Add a Company Page:

If you're marketing a business or your expertise (which is a business!), you must have a Company Page. This addition of a Company Page will allow both you and your employees to properly connect the Experience related to your organization to the Company Page. Not doing so is a serious miss in your overall branding!

The good news is that it's straightforward to put up a Page if you know where to begin!

- BE SURE THAT WHOEVER IS DOING THIS IS THE OWNER OR AN EMPLOYEE WHO IS HIGHLY TRUSTED. Viewers will forever tie it to their profile!

- Click on the Work tab at the top right of your profile.

- Scroll to the last line on the dropdown that says, "Create a Company Page."

- It will take you less than five minutes to walk through the instructions.

- Be sure that you have your logo available to upload. Similar to the personal profile banner, there's an option to upload a banner for the Company Page. Unfortunately, it's not the same size as the individual profile banner, so you'll need one that is the right size. Now is often an excellent time to involve a graphic designer or to engage your creativity. Remember that this is a prominent area of your Company Page profile, so make it pop!

- You'll also want to add a brief description of what your organization does and a tagline.

- You can add up to three hashtags representing keywords to help interested people (and LinkedIn's artificial intelligence) find you and your Page. For example, my MaxPotential U company hashtags are #careerdevelopment, #linkedinmarketing, and #personalbranding.

- From there, you'll have the opportunity to add posts, build followers and engage your employees as Brand Advocates (this is one of my favorite elements of LinkedIn as it's a little-known process and SO effective in building brand awareness for your organization from the inside out! It's also a subject that will need more discussion, so if you're interested, please reach out to me at peg@maxpotentialu.com.)

- Once you have your Company Page posted, encourage your employees, if you have them, to connect their Experience (associated with your Company) to the new Page as described above. Note that while they are your loyal employees, you have some influence over their actions. Rarely do people alter their Experience descriptions once they leave a company, so if they've been "coached" to have a compelling, complementary narrative, it will live on to advertise your brand forever!

Engagement and Activity (E&A):

These are terms used by LinkedIn (and much of digital marketing) to describe both the quantity and quality of what you DO on LinkedIn. And, for good or bad, LinkedIn shares your activity through your profile in the Activity section and through the Notifications it sends. This topic is a complete book in itself. As I'm limited on space and scope, I will offer some thoughts on how your E&A affects your brand.

- **Posting**: From your Home screen, you can enter a new post into your Feed. In 2021, LinkedIn significantly increased the available character count of posts from 1300 to 3000. This change brought a lot of chatter about why and if it was a good idea. We're finding that too much poor writing or bad messaging is terrible regardless of how long it is and, of course, the opposite. Lots of good, engaging, exciting copy gets read. So, as you post original content, write copy that your audience will care about and find compelling!

- **Engaging**: To ensure good engagement
    - Add an @ symbol in front of a person's name, or a business, that you mention in your post or comment. This addition will trigger a notification that you have mentioned them, and, ideally, they'll comment on your post.
    - Add Hashtags by putting the # symbol in front of a word or phrase that will help visitors find your post. Think of hashtags like the index at the back of a book. The addition of hashtags allows LinkedIn visitors to see what they're interested in.

BONUS.....Social Selling Index (SSI):

Another little-known and utilized (and FREE) tool that LinkedIn offers us is the Social Selling Index. Although this tool is associated with LinkedIn Navigator, a paid LinkedIn level; it's free for everyone.

What is SSI? It's a specific page with data that measures four foundational areas of LinkedIn success: Your professional brand, your ability to find the right people, how well you engage with insights, and your relationship-building prowess. Doesn't this already sound valuable?

To find your SSI scores from your computer, open up and log in to LinkedIn. Then, open a new tab and go to www.linkedin.com/sales/

ssi. This new tab will direct you to YOUR SSI scores. On mobile, log in to LinkedIn through a browser to access your SSI. (You can't get there from your LinkedIn app.) It will ask you to log in to LinkedIn using your usual password and username.

How do I use the SSI index? Regardless of whether you're a sales professional or not, the SSI can help you sell yourself and your brand!

- Start by noticing how you rank compared to others in your industry and network. These stats are just below your SSI scorecard. You might want to take a screenshot of this entire page and save it for future comparison.

- To the right of your index score is a question mark. Click on it to learn more about how you can increase that particular score. For example, the first component of your score is to Establish your professional brand. Once you click on the question mark, it goes on to explain: Complete your profile with the customer in mind. Become a thought-leader by publishing meaningful posts.

- I recommend that you go through all four topics and, again, remind yourself of your Brand Purpose. Then, prioritize which element(s) you want to focus on and create a series of action steps to help you accomplish your goal.

Before we part....

Building Your Brand of Brilliance is not a one-and-done event; it's a lifetime approach. I hope you've gained some insight into the why and what of personal marketing, brand-building, and focusing on LinkedIn.

By the time you read this, some of the LinkedIn instructions could be obsolete. That's the nature of digital platforms, but much will be the same or close. I've found that a quick Internet search can answer almost any question, so don't hesitate to continue your quest to learn and be more!

And know that I'm here as well!

Peg Stookey

Marketing, for Peg Stookey's clients (typically business leaders and career professionals), is a personal journey; often fraught with insecurity, fear, and paralysis. Even the most accomplished marketing professionals struggle with self-promotion!

Fortunately, Peg excels at helping these talented experts unearth their hidden potential, unleash it with story-rich communication, and sell their most important product: THEMSELVES!

Peg came by her marketing expertise the hard way: through PERSONAL EXPERIENCE & DILIGENT TRAINING. Her route to become a sought-after Career Change Coach and Personal Branding Strategist has been more like traversing a lattice rather than climbing a career ladder.

A biology major in college, Peg was headed into medicine to fulfill her dream of becoming a surgeon when she discovered two previously unconsidered passions: Scientific Research and Family-

Building. Working in a cell biology lab, she helped to uncover information used to treat and, one day, cure cancer, and other diseases.

But, the call to raise their four children and build the foundation of a solid family was stronger than her need to contribute to science. Peg dedicated ten years to focus on her family and, together with her husband, Mitch, to ensure their legacy of a close-knit family.

As her kids needed her less (by the way, the need never fully goes away!), she started using her innate abilities to help professionals answer the question, "What do I want to be when I grow up?" She developed her signature, Career Change Readiness coaching program, which hundreds of professionals have used since its inception.

While coaching her clients through successful career and entrepreneurial transitions, Peg increasingly saw another critical need. Her clients universally struggled to advocate for themselves. And while she recognized that she was exceptional at helping them uncover their hidden potential, she wasn't the right resource to help with their personal marketing.

Or was she?

In 2018, Peg discovered the answer in a newfound passion for Personal Branding. She trained to become a Certified Personal Brand Strategist and, knowing how important LinkedIn was to her clients' career journeys, a Certified LinkedIn Ninja Partner.

Peg's "teaching moment?" If you can't find a solution, create one!

Today, Peg's clients (a blend of small business owners and career professionals) are seeking to elevate their brand presence and create more fulfilling futures. Whether she's working with an individual career changer, a business leader, or their organization, Peg has discovered that focusing on the personal side of branding and marketing is the leader's key to attracting more of what they want and need.

To that end, in 2021, Peg completed a related certification in Career Storytelling to ensure that her clients move forward by creating compelling personal marketing assets such as optimized, story-enriched LinkedIn profiles, resumes, cover letters, and bios.

Connect with Peg:

http://www.maxpotentialu.com/

https://www.linkedin.com/in/pegstookey/

4.
Treasured Products

How The Lessons of Artists and Artisans Can Help Your Business

James Szuch, Product Development Advisor

My Story

Moving to Nashville several years ago brought a lot of changes to my life. There was a new job and a new home, new friends, new restaurants, new everything. There were also new clients and new types of clients. During more than a decade in Cincinnati, I worked with many of the city's non-profits, particularly in the arts. I worked with theater companies and art galleries and community art centers. I helped write strategic plans and build new and compelling programs.

After moving to Nashville, I found myself working more with individual artists than arts organizations. There were musicians of course, this is the Music City. But there were also photographers and painters, writers and designers, sculptors and jewelers. The jewelers brought me into the orbit of the nascent Nashville Fashion Alliance, a trade organization supporting one of the largest collections of independent fashion brands in the country. As I worked with these talented artists and artisans, I struggled with one key question: What problem do they solve?

The Problem

It isn't just an academic question. My business is solving problems. More specifically, it is helping businesses build products that deliver value by solving the important problems of their customers. To do that, I need to understand the problems those customers are trying to solve and how they measure success. And to do that, I need to understand the job the customer is trying to accomplish.

The late author and former Harvard Business School professor Clayton Christensen made the case that in order to understand what motivates people to purchase a particular product, you need to understand the job they need to get done when they use the product.[1] In his original article on the subject, he quoted another famous Harvard Business School professor, Arthur Levitt, who would famously tell his students that "people don't want to buy a quarter-inch drill. They want a quarter-inch hole!" That approach, focusing on the problem the customer wants to solve, not the product we want to sell, is now known as Jobs-To-Be-Done.

I have used the Jobs-To-Be-Done, or JTBD, approach for years to help build compelling products that solve customer problems. I've taught JTBD in my entrepreneurship classes and used it with my clients. However, sitting across the table from an abstract visual artist, I struggled to understand the job her customer was trying to do when they purchased her art to hang on their wall. They weren't just covering up a quarter-inch hole.

The Solution

My first step in solving the problem was something I had learned about years before – Maslow's Hierarchy of Needs. In order to better understand what motivates us, psychologist Abraham Maslow proposed that five basic categories of needs motivate people. These needs are physiological, safety, love, esteem, and self-actualization. You will often see these needs arranged like a pyramid. We satisfy our lower-level needs, such as the physiological needs of food and water, before focusing on the next level of the pyramid.

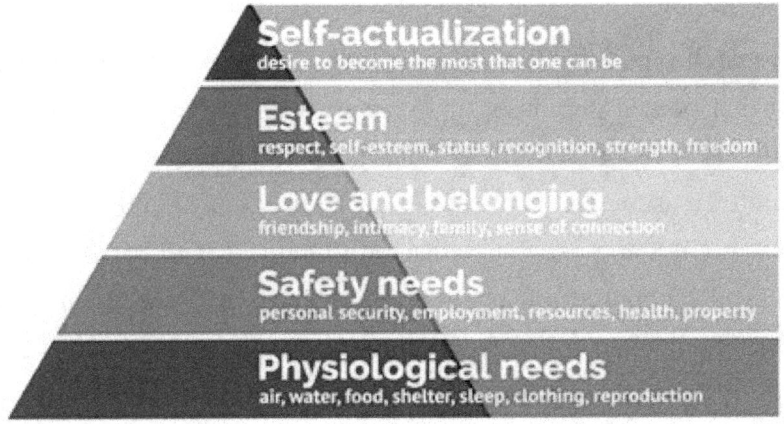

Maslow's hierarchy of needs

Purchasers of art aren't addressing their psychological or safety needs. They aren't trying to put food on the table. They are satisfying higher-order needs. They buy the art because it makes them feel good. They buy the art because they believe that people will admire them or accept them. They buy the art to satisfy emotional and social needs, not just to solve functional problems.

The Jobs-To-Be-Done approach already incorporates this line of thought. It recognizes that customers need to address different multiple jobs at the same time. The main job may be to solve a functional problem. At the same time, customers may need to solve different related jobs. Those jobs are divided into two categories: emotional and social. Emotional jobs reflect how people want to feel while performing the main job or as a result of performing it. Social jobs indicate how the customer is perceived by others while performing, or as a result of performing, the main job.

The Research

A research report published by Barclays Bank in 2012 supports the idea that people purchase art to satisfy these emotional and social needs. This report, "Profit or Pleasure? Exploring the Motivations Behind Treasure Trends,"[2] based on a survey of 2,000 rich people in over 17 countries, found that only about a tenth of the people surveyed purchased art, or other collectibles, as investments. Over 75% of them cited enjoyment as the key reason for the purchase. The report grouped the complex motivations into three major categories:

- personal enjoyment – purchasing art because of the pleasure it gives them
- social activity – purchasing art for social purposes such as sharing it with friends or showing it to others
- heritage – purchasing art because they enjoy it and want to pass it along to their descendants

The study does have a narrow demographic – individuals with more than $1.5 Million in investment assets. Anecdotal evidence supports these insights. I suspect that if you started asking friends why they purchased the art that hangs on their walls, they would give you similar reasons. So while we, or our customers, may not have the economic means to obtain actual treasures, we can still find products, services, and brands we treasure for many of the same reasons.

Not only does this study support the idea that people make purchase decisions in order to satisfy emotional and social needs, but it also shows that sometimes these non-functional needs are the primary reason for purchasing. That's a game-changer! What your product does isn't everything. You can differentiate your product and your brand by how it makes your customers feel.

But I Don't Sell Treasures!

At this point, you may be wondering why this matters to you. Unless you are an artist or a purveyor of antiques, the behavior of the treasure hunter may not seem to matter. But it does. Your business competes with dozens or hundreds or thousands of other businesses. Your business and your products need to stand out. You can apply what we learn from artists and artisans to help you not only make products that matter to your customers but products that are treasured by your customers.

In the groundbreaking book Crossing the Chasm, Geoffrey Moore writes extensively about providing customers with *acompelling reason to buy*.[3] I've always loved that phrase because of the urgency it entails. If something is compelling it can't be resisted. You want your products to be compelling. The authors of the Barclays study pointed out that:

"The emotional and social attachment to treasure means that investors are extremely likely to make sub-optimal decisions about when to buy, sell or how much to pay."

That's compelling. Understanding and addressing a customer's functional needs is important to building a product that is attractive. Understanding and addressing a customer's emotional and social needs helps you build a product that matters in ways that checking off functionality can't. It helps you build products that are treasured.

Understanding your customers' social needs, and the beliefs that underpin them is also important for your brand. In a 2018 report, the PR firm Edelman looked into the behaviors of "belief-driven" consumers.[4] This report found that a company's stand on social issues would affect the buying behavior of 64% of consumers around the world, up 13 points from 2017. That's a lot of people. Here in the United States, that number is around 57% – up 10 percentage points from a year earlier. The survey grouped consumers by how beliefs shape their buying behavior. Edelman identified three categories of consumers: spectators, joiners, and leaders. People who rarely buy on belief or punish brands for taking a stand, spectators, represented 36% of that global audience. Joiners, another 34%, will change their buying behavior based on a brand's stance on an issue. Leaders have strongly held, passionate beliefs and the brands they buy are one important way in which they express those beliefs. Leaders represented 30% of the people who responded to the survey.

Let that sink in for a moment. Look across a room of 100 randomly selected people. Thirty of those people have strongly held beliefs about some issue and make a point of buying products from companies they feel share those beliefs. Do you share their beliefs?

Do they know you share their beliefs? Do your products reflect those beliefs? Does your brand?

Treasures in the Real World
Have I Told You About My Shoes?

Fashion is a great example of the interplay between functional, emotional, and social jobs. You can buy a jacket to keep you warm and dry. That's a functional need. You don't have to spend thousands of dollars to have a custom-made leather jacket just to keep you warm and dry. But Savas, a very successful brand based here in Nashville, will make you one and they make many each year.[5] Savas jackets are treasures.

How about an example of something a bit more affordable, and pedestrian? Let's look at my shoes. Like most of you, I have more than one pair of shoes. I have shoes that I purchase for specific technical reasons – my hiking boots for example. They are waterproof, with good treads that are ideal for hiking the often slick trails to and from waterfalls here in Tennessee, and they have excellent ankle support. The majority of my shoes have less stringent functional requirements. Functionally, they just need to protect my feet and provide support. Most of those shoes, for casual or business wear, come from another Nashville company – Nisolo. Why?

While working for a development agency in Trujillo, Peru, Patrick Woodward, one of the founders of Nisolo, met a number of incredibly talented shoemakers in the city. These shoemakers were facing many of the same barriers to growth he had seen in other parts of the developing world. Most importantly, they needed access to a global market where they could sell their goods. Patrick started thinking about how revitalizing the shoe industry would impact the economy of Northern Peru. That vision grew as he began to consider what would happen if we started a fashion brand committed first and foremost to ethical production and the wellbeing of the producers. He and his co-founder, Zoe Cleary, launched Nisolo in late 2011.[6] Today Nisolo is a Certified B Corporation with a factory in Peru, a partnership with a factory in Mexico, and relationships with independent artisans in Kenya. They are committed to providing living wages to their workers and reducing their impact on the environment. I met Patrick in 2017 when his company was already successful and a key member of Nashville's burgeoning fashion industry. After hearing his story, I purchased my first pair of Nisolos – a black Oxford dress shoe.

For me, Nisolo offers a number of values that go beyond the functional needs of protection and support. They have a classic design that appeals to me. They are also manufactured and sold by a local business and one that provides benefits to society – in the way they treat their workers – and to the environment. I receive emotional value from all of those aspects of their products and their brand. I also tell people about the brand so I receive social benefits from associating myself with their products and their brand. Their products are also made of quality materials and are reasonably priced, so I don't have to sacrifice in those areas to receive emotional and social benefits other shoes don't provide.

Movements urging you to buy from ethical providers, or buy from minorities or from veterans tap into those emotional and social needs. As a customer, you receive an emotional benefit from supporting a cause or a category of business owner that matters to you. You also receive a social benefit by affiliation – by being part of a group that shares those values and who acts on them. While it may not be the primary reason you purchase a product, the value isn't trivial and is definitely part of the purchase decision.

Do You Buy "Made In America"?

Do you try to purchase products that were made in America? In the creative economy, the label "Made In America" is frequently an important element of the brand. The artists and artisans who I work with, and who are making their art and their products in their studios or workshops, are definitely making their products in America. Most of the fashion brands with which I am involved proudly support local or regional manufacturing. A 2017 article in The Sourcing Journal took a hard look at consumer sentiment about the Made in America label.[7]

The article, citing a poll that Ipsos Public Affairs conducted for Reuters, wasn't particularly cheery; neither was it particularly surprising. In a poll of 2,800 Americans, 70% felt that it was at least somewhat important for the products that they buy to be made in America. But 38% were unwilling to pay one penny more in order to support companies who did manufacture their products domestically. While more than half the people polled were willing to spend something more on products that were made in America, the number went down as the price went up. Only 3% were willing to pay 50% more and another 4% were willing to pay a 100% premium for those products. So of the more than 2,800 people polled, only 7% are willing to pay a significant premium for products that were made in America.

If you are a business that sells products made domestically, you probably aren't surprised. People may admire your work and comment on the quality, or the materials, or the craftsmanship, but they don't necessarily buy it.. Price wins out over the desire to support the local manufacturer. In that same poll, 94% of consumers considered the price to be at least somewhat important in making their decision.

The "Made in America" label is another example of an emotional or social need. Being made domestically doesn't change how the product works or what it does. The customer benefit is similar to the benefit of purchasing a shoe made ethically or by a member of a particular group. The good news of the study is that 7% of consumers value the "Made in America" label enough to pay a premium for products that reflect that emotional or social value.

While the data in the study speak specifically to the "Made in America" label, the principle is the same no matter what differentiates your product. Regardless of what you make or how you make it, there will always be people who do not value your product, or the elements that differentiate your product from competitors, enough to justify the price that you are charging for it. I advise my clients and students to stop lowering prices to appeal to those consumers. Instead, they should focus on finding the consumers who do value their product and their brand.

How Do You Make Money Providing a Free Game?

For the last example, let's look at something that has no functional benefit at all. If you are a video game player or if you have children or friends who are video game players, you probably have heard about

Fortnite. Released in 2017, it is an incredibly popular, and profitable, "battle royale" game. In this type of game, a player is dropped into a virtual world with up to 99 other players and they begin a mad dash to pick up as many items and weapons as possible, race to the center of the map killing other players as you go. The winner is the last player left alive. It sounds brutal, but with a cartoonish style, it appeals to gamers young and old; unlike the gritty, mature looks of other games of this similar style. It is also popular because the mobile version, available for Android and Apple phones, is free to play. Anyone can download the game and play it for as long as they want without paying a dime.

How do you make money from a free game? It may not cost you any money to play Fortnite, but that doesn't mean the publisher, Epic Games, doesn't make *any* money. In the game, players can purchase V-Bucks, a special currency they can use to buy emotes and skins. Emotes are dance moves your character can do within the game and skins are outfits and accessories. At $9.99 per 1,000 V-Bucks players can spend a lot on dance moves, outfits, and accessories. And Players do spend a lot on dance moves, outfits, and accessories. A May 2021 article on the website Elescpo, an online news outlet dedicated to electronic games, revealed that in 2020, the free-to-play mobile versions of Fortnite generated over $160 million in revenue.[8]

Another important aspect to understand about those dance moves, outfits, and accessories: they don't help you win the game. They are completely cosmetic. Let that sink in for a moment. In 2020, people playing a free game on their Android and Apple devices paid over $160 million to pay for things that make them look good but don't help win the game.

People value the emotional and social benefits they can obtain from the products and services they purchase. If they value those benefits, you can start providing those benefits in the product and services you sell. This will help you stand out from your competitors and command a premium price. Let's look at how you make that happen.

Uncovering the Treasure In Your Product

Now that you have an understanding of why we care about emotional and social needs, let's take a look at how to identify them and incorporate them into your products and services. The process is simple, but it will take some effort to engage with your customers and some out-of-the-box thinking to understand their needs and how to meet them. Unfortunately, I don't have the space to fully document how to plan, conduct, and assess a Jobs-to-Be-Done interview. Instead, I'm going to focus on the basic framework and emphasize the changes I make to be sure I capture those emotional and social needs. If you want more information on Jobs-to-be-Done, I suggest you take a look at Clayton Christensen's Competing Against Luck or Jim Kalbach's The Jobs To Be Done Playbook.

A word of warning here: you need to talk to your customers. You can't identify jobs by brainstorming them. Nor can you find them in marketing analytics. You are going to have to go out and actually talk to people. So, we need to identify our customers. Who are those people?

Identify Your Customers

Start with your existing customers. Even if you can't concisely articulate the jobs they are doing or the needs you are satisfying, your customers are finding value in your products. Identify your best customers and ask them to let you interview them to learn more about their needs and how you can better serve them. Who are your best customers? Repeat purchases are an obvious indicator of a happy customer and a great place to look for your best customers. Purchase metrics are one measure of customer value but not the only one. The number of referrals a customer makes is a strong indicator of how valuable you are to them. Which customers are referring your company to others? Are you on social media? Who is talking about your products to their friends and colleagues? You are looking for customers who evangelize your products and your brand.

For every customer who did purchase, there are plenty of people who didn't. These aren't the potential customers who haven't seen or heard of your amazing products. These are the prospects who saw or heard and chose **not** to purchase. Maybe the price was too high, or the time wasn't right, or the offering wasn't exactly what they needed. Regardless, their perspective on the job they are performing and what they need to perform the job is critical. You will also use this information to help you zero in on the distinctions between values that make a difference in customer purchase decisions.

How many subjects? At a minimum, you'll need to talk to at least seven people before you start seeing consistent patterns. You should try to increase that to a dozen or so to get even better data.

Have Your Subjects Prepare

To help capture emotional and social needs, I provide subjects with some homework. Ask them to provide a list of seven brands they can't live without.[9] When I was first asked to do this I pushed back a bit. There are no products or brands I *can't* live without.* *(You will need at least five brands to begin to get a picture of customer preferences. More than ten brands is more work than your customer may be willing to do and won't provide you with significantly better data. I stick with seven.)

However, there are products and brands I consume regularly; there are some brands I evangelize for. One of them is Nisolo, but that shouldn't surprise you. You want your subjects to not only identify the brands they love but the brands they treasure. You also want them to explain "why?" Why do they feel the way they do about the product or brand? What does it do for them? Have them write down their answers and submit them before the interview. The purpose of the exercise is to get them thinking about what they value in the products they buy and the brands they consume.

You'll start each interview with a quick review of this homework. If they didn't provide it to you beforehand, have them read through it now; and take notes. You are looking for commonalities, and you will find them. There will be recurring themes that will help you understand the kinds of needs that are important to your customers. You will find, as I have, that there will be some key functional elements in their descriptions – attributes like quality and price. But when you ask them about the brands, they will go on at length about the emotional and social needs of theirs that the products are satisfying. They will talk about how the brands make them *feel*. That's why we are doing this exercise. We want them to start thinking about and expressing these personal needs and talking about the products and brands that support them.

Understand Your Customer's Jobs

The interview itself is an open interview in which the subject will speak in their own words about their needs. Later you can translate what you've heard into the terms of Jobs-to-be-Done. Now you want to focus on your customer's language. It's not about reading from a questionnaire, but instead steering a conversation through specific topics. To do this, create a one or two-page discussion guide to refer to during the session. Think of it as a list of prompts for you, not a survey for your subject.

In the first part of the interview, you'll want to understand the jobs your customer is trying to do. What are you trying to accomplish by using your product? What goals or objectives does the product help you to accomplish? What problems does the product help you to prevent or resolve?

Jobs-to-be-Done considers two different kinds of jobs. The main job to be done is the primary task the customer wants to achieve. Let's explore a simple example: paper straws.[10]

Why do people use drinking straws? What are they trying to accomplish? They are trying to consume a liquid. That's the primary job. But you don't need a straw to consume a liquid. Something else must be going on.

In addition to the primary job, there could be one or more related jobs. Think of the related jobs as additional needs the user has when performing the primary job. In talking to customers about straws, we've identified two problems drinking straws solve for them. The first is reducing the mess that can be made while drinking. If you drink from an open cup or can, you can get the liquid on yourself or easily spill it into your environment. Straws are a neater way to drink. The other potential problem is reducing exposure to contaminants. Whether you are drinking from a glass in a restaurant or a can you have purchased in a convenience store, a straw gives you a cleaner way to consume.

As we've seen, there are also emotional and social jobs that your customers want to do. The emotional jobs relate to how people feel when they are doing the primary job. The social jobs are how the customer believes others perceive her. Getting to the emotional and social jobs is a bit more challenging than walking through the functions your product performs. To start, you can ask how the product makes your customer feel. That can be a little too open-ended to be practical. You need some guardrails.

In their 2016 Harvard Business Review article The Elements of Value,[11] Bain consultants Eric Almquist, John Senior, and Nicolas Bloch used Maslow's Hierarchy of Needs as a framework to explore 30 "elements of value" – fundamental attributes of products arranged into four categories: functional, emotional, life-changing, and social impact. These elements can be excellent prompts to help understand your customer's emotional and social needs. Rather than just asking "How do our products make you feel?," you can probe more directly with questions like:

- How does the product spur you to achieve your goals? (Motivation)
- How does the product help you worry less or feel more secure? (Reduce Anxiety)

- How does the product help you to become part of a group or identify with people you admire? (Affiliation and belonging)

- How does the product help you connect with other people? (Connect)

Not all the values will apply to all products. The cup of coffee I purchased this morning isn't likely to have an heirloom value (a good investment for future generations) but the coffee shop itself might have a nostalgic value (reminding me of something positive in the past). Nor is the Elements of Value list necessarily complete. We looked at the importance of supporting local businesses earlier in this chapter and you won't find a "supports local business" element in the Harvard Business Review article. But it is a good start and you can supplement it with what you've learned from other customers or from the treasured brands' assignment mentioned earlier. If you're in the business of selling to other businesses, don't despair. They have also developed a companion B2B Elements of Value framework.[12] It explores not only the needs of the organization, like managing the bottom line and achieving regulatory compliance but the needs of the individual decision-makers.

With SOStraws, we already knew that the company and the product supported the environment, so it was easy to include this as something we could talk to customers about. It shouldn't surprise you that most of the customers we spoke with identified that as a key-value they were seeking when using paper straws as an alternative to plastics. In the end, we had the following list of jobs or needs:

- Price — customers wanted straws to be affordable

- Reduce mess — customers didn't want to make a mess while drinking

- Reduce contamination — customers wanted to avoid contamination from whatever they were drinking

- Last longer — customers wanted straws that lasted longer

- Flavor impact — customers wanted straws that didn't change the flavor of their drink

- Environmental impact — customers wanted straws that didn't harm the environment

Quantify The Values

You now know what jobs the customer is trying to do as they relate to your product. You know what they value when trying to accomplish that job – functionally, emotionally, and socially. Now you need to understand how important the various values are to your customer. Now it's time to get quantitative!

For each of the jobs you've identified, ask the customer to rank how important each is to their satisfaction. I use a Likert scale for this. Likert scales are quite popular because they are one of the most reliable ways to measure opinions, perceptions, and behaviors. You've seen them. These are the survey questions that ask you to show your position on a range of discrete values, such as how satisfied you are or how important something is.

We're going to use them here to understand how important each value is to the customer. For each of the values, the customer identified, ask her to show, on a scale of 1 to 5, how important the value is in her decision. You may find it helpful to share a list of options:

1. Not at all important

2. Not very important

3. Somewhat important

4. Very important

5. Extremely important

You don't need to write out the questions. Just refer to your notes. You should record the score for each one. Later, you will summarize the data across all of your participants. When we do that for our paper straw example, we come up with something that looks like this:

Value	Importance
Price	2
Reduce Mess	3
Reduce Contamination	3
Last Longer	4
Flavor Impact	4
Environmental Impact	5

This tells me a lot about a customer. This person is not very price sensitive for straws but is very concerned about the environment. Most of the values are in the middle which I always interpret as the "I don't have a strong feeling about this" answer, but reducing mess is something a little more important. Another customer might be more concerned with price and with, for example, flavor, but not necessarily about the environment.

You have a lot of information from your interviews. Now you turn that information into knowledge you can use. Time to crunch some numbers! For each of the values, calculate the average of the customers' importance scores. I round these to whole numbers. While it may be interesting to know that the average importance of longevity across the dozen customers you spoke with is 3.71, that really isn't any different from a 4 on my Likert scale. There's a reason Likert scale values are all integers. It keeps things simple. It also tells you how important each job is to your customers and how well each of the alternatives performs in satisfying those jobs.

Looking at our paper straw example, we see that customers, on the whole, don't particularly price-sensitive, and find environmental impact to be the most important value in selecting a straw. They also value longevity and flavor impact and then reducing mess and contamination. I know what values to communicate to those customers.

Value	Importance
Price	2
Reduce Mess	3
Reduce Contamination	3
Last Longer	4
Flavor Impact	4
Environmental Impact	5

Identify Your Market

We now know some things about our customers and about what they value. But who are those customers? Is it "people who use straws"? Or is it really "people who use disposal straws"? Either works. But we can make it better. When I define a target market, I try to do it in a way that maximizes value. I look for a group of people (or companies) who are going to get the highest value from the product. As we've seen, value doesn't just come from what the product does. It comes from how it makes our customers feel. We've also seen that emotional and social value can significantly influence customer beliefs about value. It can also influence their behavior. Let's use that knowledge to identify the customers who will not only buy our product but who will treasure it.

A treasure is something that satisfies the emotional and social needs of a group of customers. SOStraw's customers value the environmental impact of their straws more than anything else. So who is their target market? People who care about the environment, particularly the oceans. They may already use paper straws or they may not be. If they care about the oceans, they will care about the SOStraws product.

Writing The Position Statement

Now that you understand what your customers value, you can draft a positioning statement that communicates that value clearly to your market. A positioning statement is a succinct statement that articulates a product's unique value to customers. Geoffrey Moore popularized a "mad lib" approach to writing product positioning statements that look something like this:

For *target customer*
who *have a specific need*
our product is a *product category*
that provides *breakthrough benefit*
unlike *competitor in the category*
we have a *compelling reason to buy*

Armed with the knowledge you have from your customer interviews and subsequent Jobs-to-be-Done analysis, you can write a powerful product positional statement to help guide your businesses. With the environmentally conscious consumers of paper straws, SOStraws can say that:

For people who care about the oceans, SOStraws offers an environmentally friendly drinking straw that, unlike other paper straws, doesn't disintegrate in your drink or add a nasty aftertaste.

The Benefits of Marketing Treasures

Product positioning statements of this form are common. What makes this one stand out is that it positions the product not just as a solution for a problem, but as something that reflects who the customer is or wants to be seen as. It defines a treasure.

It also defines the market in terms of what customers care about, not who they are or where they live, or what they need to do. Treasures transcend demographics. People of any age or zip code may care enough about the oceans to want to use a product that helps protect them. People in any income bracket may pay a higher price to do just that. We've seen that in the research about "Made in America" products. It's hard to assign a number to the value a customer receives from an emotional or social benefit.

Another benefit of defining your market this way is that it changes where you look for customers. A target market is more than just a set of customers. In order to sell to those customers, you need to find them. You seek them out where they congregate with other customers. It is best to do that where they congregate with other customers to discuss the problem you are solving or the need you are satisfying. If you are a wedding photographer, you will look for customers in online wedding planning forums. When you sell a treasure, you find your customers where they come to discuss the emotional or social need you are addressing.

Your Turn

Now that you've seen the benefit of understanding the emotional and social needs of your customers and an approach to gaining that understanding, it's time to roll up your sleeves. The values of our SOStraw customers are relatively easy to identify. People use paper straws because they care about the environment. Your customers' values may be more difficult to tease out of their responses. As I mentioned earlier, The Elements of Value article is a great guide to help you look for potential values or categories of value. Talk with your customers. Conduct the interviews and see what you can learn about them and about what they value. Perform the analysis and see how your product differs from alternatives in their eyes. Craft a positioning statement that expresses that understanding.

Don't stop there. The understanding is preliminary, and the positioning is only a draft. Now it's time to experiment! You can validate the qualitative insights you've gained from a few customers through quantitative surveys shared with your target market(s). How do demographic qualities like age or education or income impact the importance of the values? How does satisfaction vary across those different dimensions? Are there other values you should consider? Are there other alternatives you should learn about?

And what about your brand? Your brand is the collection of thoughts and feelings about your customer's experiences with your company and your products. How your customers think and feel about your brand is your brand. As you incorporate those thoughts and feelings — their emotional and social needs — into your products, you are helping to shape those experiences and guide their perspective. You are defining your brand. What else can you do to solidify in your customers' minds that you value those needs?

In his popular book, The Lean Startup, Eric Reis introduced an experimental approach to building a successful business.[13] This is a scientific approach in which we validate assumptions through experiments, usually involving live products, the results measured, and the lessons are then quickly incorporated into the next version of the product. That "build, measure, learn" loop uses the famous minimum viable product (MVP) to enable validated learning. Your understanding of customer jobs fits neatly into this loop and into the building of successive generations of your MVP. As you cycle through the loop, again and again, you will refine your understanding of your customers' needs and improve your ability to satisfy them. If you keep your eyes open to the emotional and social needs of those customers and their functional ones, you will strengthen their commitment to your brand and, hopefully, become a brand they treasure. When the next business, or businesses, asks its customers to identify seven brands they can't live without, you might be on that list.

But you need to start.

Notes

1. https://hbr.org/2005/12/marketing-malpractice-the-cause-and-the-cure
2. http://www.enograf.com/media/pdf/Profit%20ili%20zadovoljstvo%20-%20kompletan%20izvestaj.pdf
3. Moore, Geoffrey A.. Crossing the Chasm: Marketing and Selling High-Tech Products to Mainstream Customers (Collins Business Essentials) . HarperCollins. Kindle Edition.
4. https://www.edelman.com/sites/g/files/aatuss191/files/2018-10/2018_Edelman_Earned_Brand_Global_Report.pdf
5. You can learn more about Savas here: https://www.ateliersavas.com
6. https://www.thegoodtrade.com/features/interview-series-zoe-cleary-co-founder-of-nisolo
7. https://sourcingjournalonline.com/what-consumers-really-think-about-made-in-america/
8. https://www.elecspo.com/games/fortnite/how-much-does-fortnite-make/
9. You will need at least five brands to begin to get a picture of customer preferences. More than ten brands is more work than your customer may be willing to do and won't provide you with significantly better data. I stick with seven.
10. This isn't a random example. One of my clients, SOStraws, produces paper drinking straws. Their product provides a simple case study to explore emotional and social needs. You can learn more about SOStraws at https://sostraws.com.
11. https://hbr.org/2016/09/the-elements-of-value
12. https://www.bain.com/insights/the-b2b-elements-of-value-hbr/
13. https://www.amazon.com/Lean-Startup-Entrepreneurs-Continuous-Innovation/dp/0307887898/

James Szuch

James Szuch believes the first step in building a business that thrives is to build products that matter. As a consultant and business leader with over thirty years of experience, he built successful businesses based on meaningful products that solve critical customer problems. As an executive advisor and educator, James' mission is to help business owners unlock their potential to achieve success.

James loves what he does and takes pride in being able to help leaders solve pressing issues and gain the traction they need to spearhead their sustainable growth journeys. When he's not working, you can often find him doing photographing the many waterfalls in Tennessee, planning his next scuba diving adventure, or sharing his love of craft bourbon with anyone who will listen.

Connect with James:

https://jamesszuch.com

https://www.linkedin.com/in/jamesszuch/

5.
Tell Your Story and Market Your Business 21 Ways

Margee Moore & Janice Weiser, BigOrange Marketing

Just like nutritious food for a puppy, a solid marketing plan is essential for your growth. To be most effective, the plan has to be complete and balanced across many areas, and chock full of the best ingredients; like SEO, content, social media, and paid boosting. All of these things work together to nurture growth and give the energy to thrive.

If you want to see great results, consider these 21 ideas for your strategic plan. But remember, just like puppies don't become adult dogs overnight, business growth takes time. Patience and persistence are required.

Pay attention to these recommendations and they will pay off with greater visibility, better recognition, and increased leads.

1. Tell your authentic story.

Does your website tell a compelling story about your company and how it's different from the rest? Being authentic will engage visitors and keep them interested in what you have to offer. A great place to start is with the book "Building a Story Brand," by Donald Miller.

Walkthrough the steps to identify the seven parts of your customers' journey. You'll use this information to create a "brand script" that will become the basis for the content on your fresh and compelling website.

Know what isn't authentic? The use of stock photos of other people when your team isn't pictured on your site or in other marketing messages. Yes, taking time for a photoshoot of your staff in your office might feel painful or like a waste of time. It won't be. (Consider this: Our clients find that photos of their real staff on social media garner much higher engagement than other posts.) Find a photographer in your area through word-of-mouth recommendations or an online resource like Snappr.com and pick a date. You will use these photos in lots of ways to tell your story.

*BigOrange Juicy Tip:

Show your current website to friends or relatives who are not familiar with your company. Can they tell immediately what your company offers and how it would benefit them? If not, your story is not clear.

2. Know who you're talking to with personas.

Let's say you're making a promotional video—it's great quality and features happy customers extolling the benefits of your products and services…in English. What if you discover that most of your customers speak Japanese? It may be a far-fetched theory, but there are likely essential things about your customers and clients that you don't know or realize. If that's true, how can you hope to "speak their language" and make them the hero in your story and your marketing efforts?

It may seem obvious, but the best way to get to know your clients or customers better is by talking to them. Asking a half dozen of your clients a list of questions can provide great insights into the average "persona" of your buyers. Ask questions like why they chose your company, what problems your company helps them solve, and how they found out about you. This information will help you identify new customers and better explain how hiring your company can help them succeed. Sketch out rough groupings of who these people are as personas.

*BigOrange Juicy Tip:

Any time you write a post for your blog or create an advertisement, ask if or how it would appeal to one of your company's personas or address one of the problems they face.

3. Look great online with a quality website.

Not only do you have to look good, but you've also got to be good, too. Site quality and performance are important. While Google changes its algorithms for ranking often, in 2021, we know that your site's user experience has to be top-notch. Take a hard look at your site:

- Is it easy to navigate or is it too convoluted?
- Is your message clear for your target persona from step 1?
- Do visitors find what they need and not immediately "bounce" off your site?
- Does it load quickly?

- Is the structure up to snuff, with no broken links or redirects?
- Is every image optimized and labeled correctly?

At this point, the internet is filled with savvy users. You need good content that's well-written with your keyword strategy in mind to help rise to the top. Your content must answer the questions your audience is asking to be relevant.

*BigOrange Juicy Tip:

Have you looked at your site on your phone lately? If it doesn't look good there, it's time for a website overhaul.

4. Combat bounce with a quality experience.

One way to see if your website is succeeding? Bounce rate. This metric shows the percentage of visitors who land on your website and immediately "bounce" away. As in golf, you want to keep this score low. Bounce rates for each page of your website are shown in the analytics section of your website's administrative dashboard. Under 35 % is best. Google will hold a high bounce rate against you in search results because it can signal that visitors aren't finding what they're looking for on your site.

In general, your marketing plan should want to bring visitors who stay on your site and perhaps visit a page or two beyond the home page. One way to do this is to offer something enticing, like a blog post of important tips or a page with discounts or package pricing.

*BigOrange Juicy Tip:

Beat the bounce with high-quality photos on your site. Grainy or irrelevant photos can signal to visitors that they're wasting their time and should look elsewhere.

5. Lead the conversation with content.

You can't talk to every one of your current or potential clients on the phone every day, or even every week, but you can blog regularly to share your thoughts, weigh in on industry news, or offer valuable advice as part of your marketing plan.

Blog posts don't have to belong, but they should appear on your site at a regular cadence. For instance, at least two to four times a month. Here's why:

- Sales teams want to offer potential clients relevant content and answer their questions. Google wants to offer people relevant content. Your consistent blogging on topics within your company's lane packs a double punch.
- Blogging beefs up your online presence, creating new paths for visitors to find you.
- Sites with content that's recent (as well as relevant) rank better. A "set it and forget it" approach won't serve you well.
- Your competitors are blogging: you can't afford for them to be the only voice customers hear.

You don't have to write all the posts yourself. To get over the "fear of the blank page" quickly, work with one or two key people on your staff every year or six months to come up with a dozen blog topics, then decide which month to post them and who will write them. It's in your best interest to have posts with keywords relevant to your business. In other words, if you offer veterinary services, don't consistently blog about pie recipes.

Looking for blog topics? Try these:

- Short recap posts about conferences you attend
- New product launch details
- List of trends in your industry
- Employee spotlights
- Photos and description of annual corporate events
- Brief write-up of a corporate charity sponsorship

*BigOrange Juicy Tip:

Still don't know what to blog about? Ask yourself, your salespeople, or your support staff what questions customers or clients are asking, then write the answer.

6. Lure them in with a sales funnel or lead magnet.

Offer people something of value when they visit your site in exchange for their contact information. This "lead magnet" could be an infographic, a checklist, an ebook, or a video; something branded with your company name that helps them solve a problem, reframe an issue or move the needle in their work.

A lead magnet is a win-win-win. Customers learn something new, you gather a new lead, and the customers' visit to more than one page on your site adds to its validity with Google.

What could you share in a lead magnet?

- 15 simple ways to avoid cybercrime at work
- A checklist of documents clients should bring to a financial planning meeting
- An ebook on making IT work during an office move
- A round-up of favorite custom home floor plans

A lead magnet lives on your site but can be promoted through social media and by your salespeople. When people offer their contact information, be sure to collect it in some structured way. A webform could lead straight into your company's customer relationship management (CRM) system. Or the form could go to a staff member's email address. Whichever way it comes to you, this information represents valuable leads that should be collected and nurtured.

*BigOrange Juicy Tip:

People love to take quizzes. (Go figure.) If you can create an interactive quiz as a lead magnet, give it a go. Make it fun or strictly informative, but keep it relative to your business. Please, no "Find Out What Ice Cream Flavor You Are" quizzes.

7. Own your Google My Business listing.

Part of digital marketing is appealing to Google. There are a few ways to do this: one is to take a second and search for your company name in Google's browser. Just type in the name and hit "go." At the top of your phone screen, or along the right side of your browser window, what comes up in Google's information on your business:

- Your street address and phone number
- Your business hours
- Your web address
- Photos
- Reviews
- Directions to your location

Because it's so prominently displayed, you want this information to be accurate and up to date. Where to start? By "claiming" your business.

1. Open Google Maps
2. Type in your street address
3. If your business's name appears, you've claimed it.
4. If your business's name doesn't appear, click the link that says "Add this business" and follow the prompts.

You can find further instructions at https://support.google.com/business/answer/2911778?hl=en

"Owning" your listing allows you to take advantage of some powerful benefits, so jump on this task when planning your marketing. There are several methods of verifying your business listing, which is outlined here: https://support.google.com/business/answer/7107242

*BigOrange Juicy Tip:

Make sure the address on your Google listing matches your address everywhere else you share it EXACTLY. Is it the same on your website, Facebook page, LinkedIn business page? Correct inconsistencies, using the Google address as your guide.

8. Bring on the photos.

When you look at the Google listing for your business, you'll see some photos – or possibly just one photo – of your business from the street. As the owner of your business listing, you can upload as many photos as you'd like. Go ahead and post photos of your staff, your products, the inside of your office, happy clients, charity events, and so on. Keep in mind that the public can post photos of your business here, too.

*BigOrange Juicy Tip:

When you post a photo on social media, just take a few extra minutes and post the same photo to your Google business page.

9. Keep it current with Google posts.

Did you know you can post weekly updates to your Google listing? While these posts are ideal for announcing current specials or offers, you can also use them to promote your latest blog post or anything else. Each post stays live for one week and includes a clickable button so you can direct people to any location online.

Google will send you a weekly report on the number of people who have seen each photo and the number of clicks on the link. You may not see jaw-dropping results here, but these posts and clicks help with your company's Google ranking.

*BigOrange Juicy Tip:

If you have special hours on holidays, use a "Google My Business" post to keep your customers in the loop.

10. Leverage rave reviews with testimonials.

Word of mouth exerts a powerful influence. Today, online reviews act as word of mouth on a larger scale; and help with search results. Reviews also act as social proof: a phenomenon that shows people often prefer to do what others have already done.

If you aren't including reviews or testimonials of your business somewhere online, you're losing out. So how do you get reviews from customers or clients? Ask them:

- For Google or Facebook reviews, the first thing to know: It's against policy to reward people for reviews. Don't offer someone something in exchange for a review on Google. Instead, outline the steps for leaving a Google or Facebook review in writing, then use it to email or pass along to customers in a printed format. While the steps aren't difficult, technology can be a challenge for some people.

- Testimonials for your website. If a client or customer offers you a compliment, thank them and ask if they would mind leaving a review or if they would be willing to appear in a very short video testimonial. With website testimonials, you can feel free to incentivize reviews by offering something of value in return for customers' responses. Use these client kudos in a prominent spot on your site.

*BigOrange Juicy Tip:

Google will alert you via email when you receive a new review. Go to your "Google My Business" account and respond to the review. No matter if the review is good or bad, a response from your business is critical. Always be courteous.

11. Save yourself time with a CRM.

How well do you know your customers? When did you last contact them? Has someone else in your company talked to them recently? Have they signed that contract you sent over? Life is confusing enough without having to track your customers and their interactions with your staff through a haphazard collection of emails, phone calls, and sticky notes. A customer relationship management (CRM) system streamlines all the clients' data and your communications with them.

And remember all those leads heading your way through the lead magnets you created in step six? A CRM is the place to input information on leads and tracks how they are moving along your sales funnel. You've worked hard for those leads, so make sure you can capture them effectively.

CRMs can range in price from free, to hundreds of dollars a month. Ask vendors for demos and have key people on your staff weigh the pros and cons of the cost of their services. Consider how easy or difficult the software is to set up and use. Talk about what you need from the system. Many offer a wide range of benefits (like automated drip emails) for you to consider.

*BigOrange Juicy Tip:

You want contact forms from your website to flow easily into your CRM system. Talk to your web developer about the options before choosing a CRM for your business.

12. Do more with marketing automation.

We're all disappointed that we still can't commute in flying cars, but marketing automation might be the next best thing. Why? Because it helps you give every lead that comes to you the attention it deserves.

Many CRMs are capable of sending out email drip campaigns, thank-yous, birthday greetings, and automatic replies to contact requests. Use them to let potential customers know they are valuable and you will be in touch with them soon. Automation's ability to respond immediately to requests helps your company or organization seem trustworthy.

Your CRM system may also be able to assign the contact to a particular staff member and remind him or her to follow up. Automating these kinds of messages takes them off your plate so you can focus on other aspects of customer service.

Automated SMS (text messaging) is also available for you to use with customers or leads. Open rates for texts are incredibly high and can almost guarantee your message will be received: a real boon to marketing.

*BigOrange Juicy Tip:

Coordinate with your sales team so they know who is getting automated emails from the system and when. You don't want potential customers to be overwhelmed with emails and messages from the automated system and salespeople at the same time.

13. Participate in the conversations on social media.

Whether you live and die by TikTok or wouldn't touch Facebook with a 10-foot pole, social media is important for marketing. The good news is that it doesn't have to be all-consuming.

Having a presence on platforms like Facebook, Twitter, Instagram, and LinkedIn, and traffic from these platforms to your website boosts online activity around your company's name. Popularity plays a role in your Google ranking.

What to share and when? Try for a regular cadence of posts. If you blog every other week, write about each of your posts on social media twice. That action alone gives you four social media posts per month — a good start. You can repeat the same post on Twitter, Facebook, and LinkedIn. For Instagram or Pinterest, photo-based posts are best.

Video is powerful and increases the likelihood that your content will show up in followers' feeds. While the idea of creating video content may make you cringe, it's not hard to take and post a very short video clip every week. Create a YouTube channel for your company and post videos there, or broadcast them through TikTok, Instagram stories or Facebook live, or just in regular social media posts. Always keep videos very short and professional.

Alleviate the daily stress of social media by using a posting tool like HootSuite or Buffer. (your CRM may also have social media posting capabilities.) Taking a few hours to load up weeks' worth of posts in advance saves you time and eliminates that nagging feeling that social media usage may bring.

*BigOrange Juicy Tip:

On social media, viewers can message your company directly. Assign someone who will monitor these sites for messages. Try to respond to them as quickly as possible.

14. Focus on quality links.

Another way to impress Google search engines is through links to your site. If Google sees other sites pointing to yours, it makes you seem like a good source of credible information. You can find out what sites are sending visitors your way by using Google Search Console.

To begin, follow the instructions for setting up an account on the Search Console at https://search.google.com/search-console/about. As part of the setup, you will need to verify the ownership of your site. You can do this by embedding code provided by the Search Console onto your site. (Lost at this point? Ask your web developer for help.) Once the console is set up, you can see all kinds of analytics about keywords, the number of pages on your site that Google has "crawled" and stats on on-site traffic; including where visitors come from (those links mentioned a minute ago).

"How do I get links?" you might ask? Do you belong to associations or chambers of commerce that list members and their links? Could you work with partner vendors or charities you support to place links on each others' sites? Anytime someone from your company speaks at an event, exhibits at a conference, or comments on an industry article, it can create a valuable link to your site.

*BigOrange Juicy Tip:

Set up a Google Alert for your company's name. (Instructions are here: https://www.google.com/alerts.) You'll get an email whenever the name is mentioned online. It's a good way to find out where and what is being said.

15. Know your competitors and your SEO keywords.

Put yourself in potential customers' shoes by logging on to an anonymous search engine that hasn't tracked your search history, like www.duckduckgo.com. Now search for a term your customers would use to find you. Who comes up in search results first? That means their site content is optimized for search or search engine optimization (SEO). Look around that company's website:

- Does it have more or fewer pages than yours?
- How do photos and the design compare to yours?
- Is the navigation easier?
- Are there customer reviews throughout?
- Is the company using a lot of copy or a little?
- Do you see a blog or videos on the website?
- Has the company been online longer and do they have

more employees?

Try again with another search term or two. If your company ranks in the top five or six, that's great! If your rankings aren't where you would like them to be, the marketing tips in this guide should help.

*BigOrange Juicy Tip:

Do you know what terms people are using to search for your company online? Moz offers a keyword tool online (https://moz.com/beginners-guide-to-seo/keyword-research).

16. Work your website user experience.

If you're not ready for a complete overhaul, you might get a slight bump in traffic with a few adjustments to your site. Here are a few to try:

- Provide a clear call to action on every page. Do site visitors know what you would like them to do next?
- If you have a call to action button that's being overlooked, try changing its color or the wording.
- Remove oversized photos or too-large videos that may be slowing your site's load time. (A slow-loading site can hurt Google search ranking.)

Another strategy is to add a new landing page to your site. These pages are "stand-alone" that provide information on a single topic or offer. The goal of the page is to have visitors take some kind of action such as purchasing a product, making an appointment, or providing you with their contact information.

You can push traffic to a landing page on social media, through an ad, or an emailed newsletter. Keep links to other parts of your site off the landing page to minimize distractions from the sales funnel. A landing page that converts visitors into leads can be sales gold. It can also help you determine the best way to spend ad dollars. If a social media ad brought great traffic to the landing page, it could be worth repeating.

The third website move to make is adding a secure sockets layer (SSL) certificate to your site. People know they're on a site with SSL certification when the URL in the browser window begins with HTTPS (instead of HTTP). It may seem like a small thing, but it signals to visitors (and Google) that your site is secure. Talk to your web developer about adding this protection to your site ASAP.

*BigOrange Juicy Tip:

Give your website a human face by including (or updating) your team members' photos. People like to put faces to names, and you can use the headshots in numerous ways: on social media, in LinkedIn profiles, in press releases, and more.

17. Pay to play with Google Ads or paid social ads.

Paid advertising like Google Ads (formerly AdWords), LinkedIn boosting, or Facebook ads can be like a stand-alone on salespeople fertilizer in helping to boost your growth. While you're in the long game of growing your business, paid ads can give you the quick hit of immediate results.

Of course, there are watch-outs: While you can get good results for as little as $50 a day, you must track these "pay per click" ads to make sure you're spending your money in the best way possible.

Let's look at Google Ads for example: Unlike print or broadcast advertising, you only pay when someone sees or clicks on your ad. If you use the platform correctly, you can target your ad only to people who are looking for the type of product or service you offer. Clicking your ad takes the visitors to your website where you can introduce them to all your selling points.

While running Google Ads won't affect your organic rankings on Google, you can use the information from well-performing ads to polish your site and other marketing efforts. For instance, if you find that an ad with a headline that contains a certain keyword brings in more visitors than other ads, you can use that keyword in your website content, on your blog, or in your social media posts.

Like other paid online ad campaigns, Google Ads need monitoring and tweaking for the best results. If you don't have the time to oversee these campaigns, you can hire experts to do it for you.

Another alternative is to use Google Ads Smart Campaigns (formerly known as AdWords Express). This simplified version of Google Ads was designed to give small, local businesses a quick entree into pay-per-click advertising without investing too much time. You can find more information about the program here: https://support.google.com/google-ads/?hl=en#topic=7456157.

*BigOrange Juicy Tip:

Although Smart Campaigns may be easier to use, they are not as full-featured – and therefore effective – as a well-managed Google Ads campaign can be.

18. Stalking? No, retargeting!

Have you ever noticed that once you shop for something online, you start seeing ads for that wherever you go on the web for weeks afterward? You're being retargeted. The practice can work for you by keeping your brand in front of buyers and building brand recognition. When people are ready to make a purchase, they feel more comfortable buying from you.

When you can't reach a possible customer directly with your marketing efforts, a retargeted ad can be your next best bet. You can use Google Adwords or Facebook for retargeting. To take advantage of these benefits, you'll need to add a special code to your website. Ask your web developer, or our team, if you need help with setup.

If you run a Google campaign, your retargeted ads can show up on a wide variety of websites or platforms. Facebook ads, of course, only appear when visitors go to Facebook.

With Google AdWords retargeting, you can specifically choose websites where your ad will run and whether you will be charged by the ad view (impression), click, or website conversion.

Facebook can show your retargeting ads in a range of places on their site. You can choose your ideal customers' demographics so only those most likely to be interested in your services see your ads.

The campaign you create specifies what will trigger a retargeting ad. For instance, visitors to your services pages would begin to see your retargeted ads after leaving your site. When visitors see your ad copy highlighting that specific service, they will be reminded of your company's capabilities.

Once that prospect becomes a lead, you can take them off the retargeting list, and move them to your automated marketing or your salespeople for further nurturing.

***BigOrange Juicy Tip:**

Don't serve up the same ad to someone more than three times. You want people to be intrigued, not annoyed, by your brand.

19. Set the goal in Google Analytics.

Most likely, Google Analytics is running as a plug-in on your website. You may even look at it on occasion for more information about how many people are visiting your site, what search terms they're using, and what other sites are sending them to yours. Another helpful tool in Google Analytics is "Goals."

With "Goals," you can define what actions you would like people who visit your site to take, like signing up for your e-newsletter or scheduling a call with your salesperson. Instructions for setting up goals are here: https://support.google.com/analytics/answer/1032415?hl=en. You can use a template or create your own marketing goals. You can even assign a dollar value to goals (by comparing ad costs vs. leads, for instance). Go to the "Conversions" tab in Google Analytics to see the data compiled.

*BigOrange Juicy Tip:

It's a good idea to create a goal in terms of conversions. Conversion rate is the most important key performance indicator (KPI) for your site because it helps you know if you are on track with your business.

20. Make news.

You might think your work is not particularly newsworthy, but members of the media often need help to decipher topics related to your expertise. "Help a Reporter Out" (HARO), is a three-time daily newsletter that connects reporters with subject matter experts. Skim the newsletters for queries you could answer in your area of expertise. If the reporter uses you as a source, your name and company name will be published. This creates valuable backlinks or online mentions and bolsters your leadership credibility.

To start using the service, register at www.helpareporter.com. Consider outsourcing the monitoring of these requests to a junior person on your team or an affordable virtual assistant, so that the daily emails don't become overwhelming.

*BigOrange Juicy Tip:

Look for ways to share with local media news about your company through press releases, too. Topics to cover include new hires, acquisitions, talks given at conferences, new certifications, awards won, or contributions your company has made to a charity. See if your local newspaper has a means for you to submit articles directly, and include captioned photos whenever possible.

21. Spread your story with webinars.

While it may seem daunting at first, hosting a webinar doesn't have to be complicated or overly time-consuming. Use a platform like Crowdcast or Microsoft Teams to host the webinar. Keep it short to retain audience interest, but leave time at the end of the Webinar for questions. You can incentivize attendees to stay engaged by pulling names for a giveaway at the tail-end of your presentation.

Practice your webinar with a colleague and, if possible, have someone else on hand to keep track of questions from attendees. Publicize your seminar on LinkedIn and through your email newsletter to clients and potential customers. Record your webinar to start building a library of resources. Your salespeople can send links to the webinars to prospects, reinforcing your role as quality service providers.

*BigOrange Juicy Tip:

Not sure how to pick a webinar topic? Think about the types of questions your salespeople or customer service people answer most often. Addressing those questions will provide your audience with value.

Tackling these 21 steps could easily feel overwhelming, but take heart in the fact that this process is a marathon, not a sprint. With all your other responsibilities, it's wise to choose just a few to take on (or delegate to others) at once. Discuss with your leadership team which steps could make the biggest impact in your organization right away.

Of course, the option to outsource this work is always on the table. In fact, you can use these 21 steps as you interview and narrow down potential marketing agencies. Would they take on all these tasks for you? Are there some you'd like to keep in-house? A clear explanation of your needs and expectations will go a long way in creating an effective partnership with an agency.

At BigOrange Marketing, we're always happy to talk about how digital inbound marketing can make a difference for small to mid-sized companies. Reach out to us for a consultation by visiting www.bigorange.marketing.

Margee Moore and Janice Weiser

As co-founders of BigOrange Marketing, Margee Moore and Janice Weiser love to share digital marketing and social media insights that help American businesses get leads and grow.

Leveraging her extensive background working at leading digital marketing agencies, Moore launched BigOrange Marketing as a woman-owned firm in 2017 to support the underserved small to mid-sized business market.

With many years of business-to-consumer and business-to-business writing and editing, Weiser oversees content for BigOrange Marketing's clients.

BigOrange specializes in IT services/MSP marketing, manufacturing marketing, builder/developer marketing and marketing for financial services firms. BigOrange ranks as a top Cincinnati marketing firm according to DesignRush and top web design firm according to the

Cincinnati Business Courier. Most of all, we pride ourselves on retaining and building long-term relationships with clients, many of whom have become friends. We are StoryBrand Certified and hold Google Analytics and multiple HubSpot certifications.

Connect with Margee and Janice:

https://www.bigorange.marketing

Margee: https://www.linkedin.com/in/margeemoore/

Janice: https://www.linkedin.com/in/janicebrewster/

6.

The 7 Key Pieces Of The Digital Marketing Puzzle

Dan Hahn, Main Street Marketing

There is a core group of online marketing activities that provides results together that none of them can provide on their own or in phases. This core group of online marketing activities provides a true internet presence that will create better search engine rankings, more engagement on social media, and ultimately more leads for small businesses.

REMEMBER… "If your prospects can't find you on the internet then you don't exist" and "If your current customers aren't inspired or prompted to take action, they'll take less of it." The following will explain what the seven key pieces of a digital marketing puzzle are and why small businesses need to use them.

#1 – A Website With Consistent Content Creation

Content is King. Nothing works online without it. Websites, Search Engine Optimization, Social Media, and Email marketing will have no effect without good content. Prospects and customers are scouring the internet looking for ways to improve their businesses and content is the way to get them interested in your products and services. Once you prove that you are a thought leader, those decision-makers will keep coming back. Once the relationship is made, the sales will come.

Remember that a website is something you own and have control over. Many small business owners use mainly just social media to market themselves and think that is enough. Putting all your eggs in one basket leaves small businesses out in the cold whenever Facebook, Instagram, LinkedIn, Twitter, or some other social media company changes their algorithm or starts charging for things that used to be free. You need the following types of content on your website to be shared in your social media, email marketing, and other marketing channels.

Search Engine Optimized Posts – These posts will get you ranked on the first couple pages of Google when specific queries are asked by your prospects. If they search for answers on a topic but don't find your posts or pages on that topic, then you are not going to get a look, an email, a call, or anything when it comes time for them to pick their favorite vendors.

Featured Work Posts – Prospects don't want you to tell them how great you are, they want to see it. They want to see before and after pictures and videos. They want to see good reviews for those specific jobs. The prospects want to know how you helped your customers. THEY WANT PROOF! If you don't show it, prospects will move on to the next company with a website that does show it.

Pictures – Pictures are great for blogs and on pages of your website. Visuals are essential for creating featured work posts.

Video – If a picture tells a thousand words, then how many words are told in a video? A bunch! Videos are quickly becoming a must-have for marketing, even for small businesses. There are ways to create videos with raw footage, pictures, and motion graphics that now make it affordable for small businesses to use video in their marketing plan. One of the easiest ways to create video is to capture conversations using Zoom or some other virtual meeting software. These conversations will give a marketing team great raw material to create a large video or smaller bite-sized videos about particular topics from your main conversation.

Podcasts – People are in their cars a lot. Podcasts are the perfect way to get decision-makers to believe in you and your company. You can use the audio from conversations you recorded on Zoom or other virtual meeting software. If you are doing this by video already, then use the audio portion for your podcasts. Speaking about specific topics and challenges just by yourself is also a perfect way to convince future prospects that they need your products and services to solve their problems.

#2 – Search Engine Optimization (SEO)

Not getting found online can break a business in this day and age. Anybody who tells you that SEO is dead is just "Loony Tunes." Over the past five years, Google has made many changes to its algorithm and we expect even more changes as Google continues its quest to give the best answer(s) to specific questions via its search results.

Your website needs to be a storage place for all your content and it needs to be easily searchable and smartly categorized. The content on your site also needs to be shared with your social media pages and profiles. The content on your website needs to be optimized for search engines. You need a combination of search engine optimized posts and featured work posts on your site to educate prospects and prove that you can do what you say. On top of this, you need good on-page search engine optimization and the right types of web pages that represent all your services, niches, and service areas. If you prove to Google that you are a good place to send their customers, you will get more traffic to your website, and if your website is good enough to convert you will get more leads.

Signals to Google That You Should Rank Higher In Their Search Results...

Fresh Content – Things are moving quickly these days, and content needs to be fresh to be correct and trustworthy. If your posts are dusty and not consistently updated, then Google won't be in a hurry to move you up in the rankings.

Mobile-Ready Content – Your content is going to have to look good on PCs, tablets, and smartphones to be valued by Google.

Transparent Unbiased Thorough Content – If your content comes across as promotion-heavy, sales copy-like, or showing only one side of things, then it's not going to be valued by Google. Content that delves into issues head-on and with a personality will get higher rankings.

Content with Multimedia – Content with multimedia (video, graphics, and/or audio) will get better rankings than blogs with only words and images. All should be optimized for SEO and the individual pieces can be used on separate marketing channels, as well as together for a cumulative effect for those who are absorbing your content.

Social Media Activity – Google will value companies who share social media posts that are linked back to their web pages and posts.

Time on Site – There may not be a better way to see if people are using your content than how much time they spend on your site. Videos and posts can really improve time on site.

Low Bounce Rate – If searchers are staying on your site after checking it out, then your content is hitting the mark for "good educational content."

Inbound Links – Links are important but they have been and continue to be manipulated. They are a signal but will continue to be devalued by Google's algorithm over time.

Strategically, the marketing world feels like it's becoming more simple in some ways. To be overly simple, you now need a website with great content that is also integrated with your social media channels. You also need a lead generation system with email marketing and email campaign capabilities. Marketing magic happens when you find the right mix for your company and it's our belief that almost all small businesses need help with creating the marketing pieces (especially the content) and finding the right marketing mix.

#3 – Local SEO

Local SEO is how you are found in searches that also take into consideration the area you are in during the search. Most of the time, it's because we are searching with our phones and the search engines know where we are when we make the search. The search engine then gives the best results back to the searcher using information that is on different social media, directories, and maps. You want to make sure you have all the right information about your company on Google, Bing, Yahoo, and 50+ other of the largest directories so that the search engine can look, find, and compare the info on them all. If your company's information is available and consistent throughout, then your company will show up higher in the local search results. Do you have better reviews that are more consistently added online than your competitors? That's a signal to Google that you should rank higher. Do you have your service areas and property business categories in all the relevant social media and directories for your industry? That's a signal to Google that you should rank higher. Are you posting your latest blogs and videos to social media? That's a signal to Google that you should rank higher. Local SEO is about having the same correct information on all those right sites and adding to those sites consistently.

Many searches never leave the search engine results page these days. This is because of the information that businesses are adding to their Google Business Profile. THIS IS A GAME CHANGER for search engine optimization (SEO). Local SEO has never meant so much to a small business and never has one company's platform (Google Business Profile) had so much sway over which business gets seen and which business does not. The following explains briefly what needs to be done to rank well locally.

- Optimize Your Google Business Profile
- Choose your Google Business Profile categories properly

- Decide the relevant keywords to use through the listing
- Optimize your website
- Report competitors that are breaking guidelines
- Confirm that directory citation information is correct
- Fill out all your Google Business Profile fields
- Collect customer reviews (and reply to them)
- Consistently Make Posts to your Google Business Profile
- Consistently add images and videos to your Google Business Profile
- Consistently answer questions from prospects/clients and post owner Q&As on your Google Business Profile

#4 – Social Media Marketing

Social Media allows you to communicate to your prospects and customers just like email but it has two very important attributes that email marketing does not. Social media allows for a two-way conversation with your prospects and customers. It also allows you to have your messages spread virally to people who are liking, following, or connecting with you on social media. You share your message with them and they can share the message with their networks and on and on. All of your search engines are optimized posts and featured work posts should be shared on Facebook, Instagram, LinkedIn, Twitter, Google Business Profile, and more on an ongoing basis. The goal of sharing posts is to educate, boost your brand, get interaction, and increase your reach to other prospects through those you already interact with.

#5 – Lead Generation/Email Marketing

Lead Generation and email marketing come into play when people start showing up to read the content on your website. They come to your website through search engines, email marketing, and social media updates. Through offers, web forms, and analytics you can see who is interested in your content. When a prospect or customer shows interest in a specific topic and takes some kind of action, you can have a triggered email sent to them to help push them through the sales funnel. It's always about getting the right message to the right people at the right time!

You can also communicate and brand your company to your prospects and customers through monthly e-newsletters. In addition, you could send monthly focused e-blasts at the start of each month promoting the services or products customers should be thinking about for a specific month. You can also let them know if you are running any specific promotions.

If your content is good and helpful, people will stay subscribed. These email marketing efforts amplify your networking efforts and help your sales team and company spread the word to large pools of prospects and customers on a regular basis.

Other Ideas for Lead Generation…

Develop Online Offers – Something of value. Not a free consultation. We are trying to get as many people in the sales to funnel as possible. We want a soft yes. A free consultation (A.K.A. sales call) is a hard yes. What can you offer that will educate your target market as to why they should be buying from you instead of your competition? Explain the apples AND the oranges between what you are offering and what your competition is offering.

Create Lead Bait – Lead bait could be industry-specific case studies, whitepapers, buying guides, etc. The headlines to these pieces of lead bait are key! Take your time on lead bait production and it will pay off down the line over and over.

Send Lead Generation Campaigns – Lead bait collects the contact information and when you have the contact information, then it can trigger educational email campaigns to begin. Now you have their ear and you can begin educating them.

Website Copy Needs to be Customer-centric – Make sure to double-check the copy of your site to make sure it's all customer-centric. Answer their questions, ease their worries, explain how you do business. Getting down in the weeds and explaining what you do in detail isn't what your prospects want. They want their problems solved for a reasonable price. They don't care that you are a "captain of industry"! It's not about you… it's about them. Show the benefits, not the features. Stay away from brochure-speak or business jargon.

"About Us" Needs to Explain Why You Are Better Than Your Competition – Next to your "Home" page, your "About Us" page gets the most traffic on your website. You need to be very clear with your prospects about your unique selling proposition. Take your time here. Show your key personnel off here and provide how to contact them.

Backup Your Assertions With Online Reviews and Featured Work Posts – Make sure to get 3rd party, online reviews and show them on your website. From the good online reviews, create some featured work posts explaining what the customer wanted, what you did for them, and the results. Pictures and/or videos, as well as reviews, should also be added to the featured work posts. Like it or not, you are presumed guilty before innocent so online reviews and featured work posts are key to gaining trust!

Video, Video, Video! Did I Say Video?! – Words are great, a picture is worth a thousand words, and video is an educational nirvana! Find the budget!!!!! There are affordable ways to do video these days.

Remember That These Tips Don't Matter If You Can't Get Traffic to Your Website – You need a mix of online and offline marketing tactics to get people to your site. Below is what *Main Street Marketing* believes are the best ways to draw traffic to your website and in this order…

1. Networking (1-1, Group, Events, Etc.)
2. Website
3. Online Reviews
4. Content Marketing (Blogs, Featured Work Posts, Videos, Lead Bait & More)
5. Social Media
6. Search Engine Optimization (included Local SEO)
7. Lead Generation / Email Marketing
8. Search Engine / Social Media Advertising
9. Everything Else

#6 – Online Review Management

3rd party online reviews (ie. Google, Facebook, etc.) prove you are as good as you say you are. In countless studies, a majority of people say that they trust online reviews as much as a recommendation from someone they know. Online reviews now affect your search engine optimization, especially your local SEO efforts. They really help convert prospects into customers. The problem is that most companies don't have enough online reviews and a frustrated customer is more motivated to post a review than someone who is happy. An online review system will make sure you get more and better reviews, just the way Google wants it.

Social media, search engines, and popular review sites allow consumer opinions to travel faster and reach further than ever before. Reviews are modern-day word-of-mouth marketing posted on sites like Yelp, Google, Angie's List, and more. Reviews are easily seen and shareable and are probably the most important aspect of marketing for small and local businesses that don't have large brand advertising budgets. Good reviews will affect people's decision to buy from your business and will increase your search engine rankings.

Why Reviews and a Review System Is Needed…

Reviews Improve Search Engine Optimization – A real review from a real person on a third party site that has some authority is a very powerful signal to Google that your business is ready from prime time and a place to send their searchers. Good reviews are a way for local businesses to get higher search rankings and compete with larger companies with deeper pockets for SEO help.

Stop Negative Reviews From Being Over Represented – An American Express study found that 9 out 10 tell people about their service experiences. Millennial customers tell an average of 17.5 people about good experiences and 14.7 about bad ones. Older customers on average tell 7 people about good experiences and 16 about bad ones.[1] So it's basically a numbers game to get the right perceptions in front of your customers. You need a larger group of people reviewing your business to stop any negative reviews from being overrepresented.

A Review System is Needed – It's tough to get a handle on getting customers to give you good reviews on social media and review sites that matter for your business. To get a good number of positive reviews you will need to commit to a strategy and use proven tools and tactics to succeed. Yes…sometimes good reviews just happen but you want to create a reviews system that gets positive reviews in an easy and unobtrusive way that asks and reminds your customers to review your business. Your review system needs to:

- Provide a way for businesses to ask and remind customers to share their experience online
- Drive customers to a destination that is designed to convert them into reviewers
- Guide reviewers to select the best possible review site for your business and then write a review

#7 – Video Production / Graphic Design

Video outperforms written content on its own every time. Videos increase your search engine rankings and website conversions.

Videos are easy to share on popular social media platforms and between interested prospects. So, why are there so many small businesses out there still not using video? We think it is because producing videos feels open-ended and costly to small business owners. Small businesses need fixed-cost pricing and concrete deliverables.

Some Video Marketing Stats…

- Dr. James McQuivey of Forrester Research says that a one-minute video is worth 1.8 million words (about 3,600 web pages).[2]
- According to ComScore, which measures online engagement and use, 45.4% of Internet users view at least one video online every month.[3]
- 75% of executives told Forbes that they watch work-related videos on business websites at least once a week.[4]

75% of executives watch work-related videos at least once a week! This statistic tells most small business owners all they need to know about video. Create a video or video series, and you can engage with busy executives who are specifically looking for solutions to their problems. Executives aren't going to surrender an hour to hear your presentation, but they'll give you 60 seconds or less to try to catch their attention. This 60 seconds could get you a meeting or close them right there and then!

Small Businesses CAN Play the Video Marketing Game With The Following Types of Videos...

- **Topical Self-Generated Video** – Have key staff make videos (usually under 3-5 minutes) that educate your prospects about what you all do for your clients. Don't worry about video quality. If you are providing informative and helpful videos, the amateur nature will be fine and sometimes even will produce more trust. Err on the side of a good microphone. Your clients have to be able to hear what you say.

- **Explainer Videos** – Explain how your products or services help companies to solve their problems.

- **Frequently Asked Questions** – All companies get the same questions over and over, so why not answer them with a video?

- **Questions That Should Be Asked** – Frequently Asked Questions' more informed cousin.

- **Profile Videos** – Remember…use real people talking like real people. Be entertaining and educational.

- **Case Studies/Featured Work Videos** – Show people your product or service in action. Show clients how other companies use your products and services.

- **How-To Videos** – Show people how to use and interact with a new product or service.

So those are the 7 Key Pieces Of The Digital Marketing Puzzle. It's really the 7 Key Pieces Of The ORGANIC Digital Marketing Puzzle.

We left out Search Engine / Social Media Advertising because it's frankly too expensive for most small businesses that don't already have a thriving business. We also feel that if you don't have the content on your site or a website or good reviews or featured work posts, then the online users who find you by an ad and come to your site to learn more are going to be underwhelmed. We are sure some Search Engine / Social Media Advertising-centric companies will disagree but that's where we stand. Now, please don't think that we don't value Search Engine / Social Media Advertising because we do. We love it but only after you have your organic marketing ducks in a row and after you have enough of an advertising budget to make a difference. Once you do, then you can check your organic analytics to see where you are coming up short and use advertising to fill in the gaps. They work best together!

Search Engine / Social Media Advertising

Once you get a handle on both networking and organic marketing, then you have the option to go after keywords you are having a tough time placing well for using just organic marketing using Google Ads. You can retarget those who are visiting your site or taking some type of action on your website on Facebook, LinkedIn, or Instagram. Then you would have all three major types of marketing building and feeding off of one another. Once you have established your Internet Presence (organic marketing), and you are going for the more non-reachable fruit, Google Ads can be a great strategy. With the right budget, Google Ads and Social Media Advertising/Retargeting will increase the results of both your ads and your Internet Presence. Just make sure you have a professional to manage your advertising program or you will be wasting money due to your inexperience. The small management fee is worth it every time.

A Professional Ad Manager Can Help You...

- **Increase Your Conversions** – The reason you are advertising is to increase your sales/leads.

- **Decreasing Your Cost Per Click** – Reviewing your current campaign and finding ways for you to pay less per click.

- **Increase Your Click-Through Rate (CTR)** – Low CTR's are due to incorrect targeting, poorly written ads, and irrelevant ads.

- **Increase Your Quality Score** – Analyzing your campaign to find why your QS is so low for certain keywords and finding ways to increase them.

- **Decrease Your Cost Per Conversion** – The main goal is for you to pay less for each sale/lead over time.

Types of Search and Social Advertising...

Search Advertising (Google) – Google is the 800-pound gorilla in search and everybody knows it. If you want to show up in search, you had better work on your organic marketing to place you on the right pages. Google ads are a great choice when you need to show up quickly in search results or when you are trying to get leads in a saturated industry; like attorneys or landscapers. Your customers are using Google every day so if you manage a restaurant that deals with the public or are a business-to-business services company that wants to reach the highest levels of management with their ads, you want to be on Google's first couple of pages for particular keyword searches.

Social Advertising (Facebook, Instagram, LinkedIn)

- **Facebook** is important because they have over 2 billion active users and they spend several hours per week or more on it. Your customers are on Facebook no matter if you manage a restaurant that deals with the public or a business-to-business services company that wants to reach the highest levels of management with their ads. The cost per thousand (CPM) impressions on Facebook is somewhere between $5-10, which makes it a very inexpensive advertising platform.

- **Instagram** has 800+ million monthly users. The photo/video-centric platform is one of the most used mobile platforms throughout the world. Since Instagram is owned by Facebook, businesses who advertise through Instagram will have access to the most robust advertising targeting system on the Internet. 75% of Instagram users take action on ads that they see on their news feed and over 1/3 of Instagram users have used Instagram to purchase a product online.

- **LinkedIn** has 550+ million users and they are a more professional and educated audience than some of the other platforms. LinkedIn is the best platform for advertising to decision-makers and high-level executives. You are allowed to target by occupation, job title, location, and many more features. You are also able to advertise to recent website visitors, as well as email contacts that are in your database. 94% of B2B marketers use LinkedIn to market their business in some capacity.

Analytics

It goes without saying that you need to check your analytics for all The 7 Key Pieces Of You Digital Marketing Puzzle and Search Engine / Social Media Advertising activity. The best marketing companies are going to be able to provide you with one dashboard to show you all of your SEO, Social, Email, Review, and Search Engine/ Social Media Advertising statistics. It's best that these statistics are something that you can check in on with login or click of a link. Monthly analytics are OK but dynamic up-to-the-minute stats are better.

Selecting a Marketing Company To Work With

We know from experience in dealing with small businesses that if marketing companies set up the system for the small businesses and then let them fill it with content on their own… it will almost certainly not get done. At best their content will be added in spurts and then left to gather dust for a while. By outsourcing your marketing to a digital marketing company that involves you in all major decisions, your key staff can devote more time to do what they do best!

We feel strongly that the digital marketing quarterback is someone who is with you in the trenches week to week. Not just somebody who works up a marketing plan and checks in with you quarterly. The best digital marketing quarterback is the person who is working on your website, creating your content, posting your social media, sending email marketing, etc. Branding and marketing strategy can be the responsibility of the digital marketing quarterback or they can incorporate strategy and ideas created in tandem by company executives and their brand marketing team.

It's also our experience that it's best to have one marketing company be the quarterback for all your digital marketing. This way all the marketing channels are rowing in the same direction. This way you have one person to contact who will have or can get all the answers you need to make decisions.

It's best for the small business to have one dedicated contact for the digital marketing quarterback to work through. In most cases, this person is more of a coordinator. Coordinating within the small business to gather what their online marketing company needs to provide the best results. This person needs to be reachable and not extremely busy. This person is usually not the CEO or owner. This person is the person who blocks the door and tells the CEO… "I need such-and-such from you for our marketing or I'm not letting you out this door!" They will be reaching out to service staff to make sure they are taking before and after pictures and video that is needed for featured work posts and so on. They are coordinating all the raw materials the digital marketing quarterback needs to market the small business in the best way possible.

About Main Street Marketing

Main Street Marketing can be the digital marketing quarterback for your small business. We help you with The 7 Key Pieces of the Digital Marketing Puzzle and when you are ready for Search Engine /

Social Media Advertising, we can help. We can also provide analytics for everything we are doing for your company.

(859) 904-8035

https://main-street-marketing.com

Notes

1. https://templatelab.com/american-express-study/
2. Larry Alton, Business.com, 7/14/2015, https://www.business.com/articles/a-one-minute-video-is-worth-1-8m-words-content-marketings-newest-weapon/
3. Daniel, InfographicPlaza.com, 5/6/2015, https://infographicplaza.com/whats-the-market-for-online-video/
4. Bill Millar, Forbes.com, 2010, https://images.forbes.com/forbesinsights/StudyPDFs/Video_in_the_CSuite.pdf

Dan Hahn

Dan Hahn's single goal, since he founded Main Street Marketing 2006, was to create online leads for small businesses. Main Street Marketing creates a comprehensive Internet Presence using the following...

- A Website With Consistent Content Creation
- Search Engine Optimization (SEO)
- Social Media Marketing
- Lead Generation / Email Marketing
- Online Review Management
- Video Production / Graphic Design
- Search / Social Advertising
- & More

This core group of services provide results together that none of them could provide on their own or in phases. They are everything a small business needs to create online leads.

Main Street Marketing's "Skin" Is In The Game, Week In and Week Out

Dan believes that small business marketers shouldn't just strategize about marketing for their clients; they should also execute their marketing plan for them. He believes that small business marketers need to be in the trenches with their customers week in and week out as they grow their businesses. Dan knows that if Main Street Marketing creates and executes a client's marketing, they will be able to devote more time to their core business tasks and concentrate on what they do best!

From years of experience dealing with small businesses, Dan knows that if he sets up a marketing strategy and a system for clients and then leaves them to create and distribute their own content... it will almost certainly not get done. At best their content marketing will be done in spurts or left to gather dust for long periods of time. No content or sporadic content and poor distribution is a recipe for bad search engine optimization.

One Point of Contact For All Your Small Business Needs

Other marketing companies specialize in just Search Engine Optimization (SEO) or Social Media or Email Marketing or Websites or Video, etc. Main Street Marketing manages all aspects of your online marketing. Providing you with just one point of contact and "one back to pat or one throat to choke!". This makes our service affordable and manageable, knowing most small business owners don't have the time or funds to manage and pay multiple marketing service providers. Having more than one person managing the marketing plan will result in diluted results from all marketing efforts. Having one point of contact managing your marketing plan, will ensure that all your marketing channels are headed in the right direction at the right times.

Contact with Dan:

http://www.main-street-marketing.com/

https://www.linkedin.com/in/danhahn/

7.

Getting Started with Digital Analytics and Dashboards

Matt Booher, Digital Analytics Expert

Introduction

Digital analytics combines the technical skills needed to successfully create online marketing with the business and statistical analysis skills needed to improve and optimize progress toward an organizations' goals. Digital analytics is the collection and analysis of the data generated by online marketing activities. More broadly, it also includes the decisions made to adjust those online marketing activities based on the conclusions drawn from the data.

For large organizations, digital analytics may be an extensive, complex, and involved program cutting across multiple departments bolstered by multimillion-dollar budgets and sophisticated tracking and marketing automation tools. For smaller to medium-sized organizations, including those run by a single individual, digital analytics efforts could be as simple as monitoring a business presence on Google and analyzing reports coming from Google Analytics about a website. But regardless of the scale of a digital analytics program, there are some consistent basics that you can apply to uncover compelling insights and ensure digital marketing success.

But before reaching too far into understanding more about digital analytics, it's also essential to understand its limitations. Appropriate digital analytics implementations respect privacy and, even in an attempt to collect the smallest amount of data, ask that potential audience and customers agree to it. Even after an agreement, most of the information collected will remain anonymous until a potential customer becomes a paying customer or verified prospect.

Conversions

So, what is a conversion? A conversion in digital analytics terminology describes the moment a visitor converts from one status to another. This moment could be the moment a prospect changes to a customer or a non-subscriber becomes a subscriber. What it comes down to is, the person goes from A to B in a way that is meaningful to the business.

Determining a conversion is as simple as identifying marketing priorities and the outcomes to be achieved from digital marketing. When running an e-commerce business, conversions occur when a customer purchases from the site or other location. When running a consultancy, a conversion might arise when someone visits the website and completes a form requesting additional information about services and/or costs. When running a service business, a conversion could occur when someone schedules an appointment online, or contacts via email or a phone call requesting an appointment conversation can take many forms depending on the nature of the business and the strategic intent of the marketing campaigns, conversions can take many forms. The key is making sure the conversions used as part of the digital analytics work focuses on the most critical outcomes. Just because someone reads an "About Us" page or clicks on a link from an email, the task of converting the individual doesn't necessarily mean the task of converting that individual is finished. Defining conversions requires deep thinking about the status changes at the heart of digital marketing.

Common conversions include:

<u>E-commerce sale(s)</u>

- Email submission(s) for newsletter subscription(s)
- Form completion(s)
- Scheduling an appointment or meeting
- Download(s) for a file or e-book
- Sharing a link or digital resource (video or email, for example) with a friend

Conversions to Key Performance Indicators

Digital analytics programs begin and end with the concept of Key Performance Indicators – or KPIs. They form the foundation of any well-thought-out web analytics program and link the data collection and analytics back to the objectives of the business. KPIs track the overall health of online marketing efforts. They help determine if those marketing efforts remain on track or need to be course-corrected. KPIs provide insight into the efficacy of the marketing efforts and how to improve conversions or other goals.

Good KPIs should tie back to conversions and:

1. Stand alone as a measure of success. A good KPI should, at a glance, provide a positive or negative assessment of the digital marketing efforts without the need for additional data or analysis. For example, a KPI such as cost per sale or cost per lead can provide quick directional guidance on whether marketing spending yields a positive impact. If the cost per sale or lead exceeds the value of the customer transaction (another possible KPI), the current marketing plans and efforts will lead the company into the red or drive incremental and accretive revenues for the organization.

2. Make sense to a business leader or investor. A robust KPI isn't laden with technical or industry-specific jargon that requires specific expertise to understand or interpret. It should be based on common business terms such as sales, revenue, customer counts, or other marketing-related outcomes specific to the business, such as form completions, email signups, etc.

3. Consistent. Good KPIs provide long-term benefits and insight into marketing performance. KPIs should not change regularly; therefore, they provide the ability to compare day-over-day, week-over-week, month-over-month, year-over-year (or any other period of time) meaningful to marketing activities and plans.

Common KPIs include but are not limited to: cost per sale, cost per lead, conversion rates for sales, leads, or other key marketing outcomes (we'll get into conversions and conversion rates in a moment), abandonment rates, and interaction rates. Once equipped with an understanding of conversions and the relationship with KPIs, digital analytics can move to focus on the technical aspects of setting a strong measurement program.

A Technical Note

It is essential to know how things work behind the scenes. While technical expertise isn't necessary to understand or work with digital analytics, understanding the technical details will help inform KPIs, what specific aspects of the digital marketing plan to track, and better appreciate the limitations of digital analytics so that measurement expectations remain realistic. There is no avoiding technical issues when it comes to digital measurement, so even the slightest understanding can have a profound impact in determining how to best measure marketing efforts.

Digital analytics data gets collected in one of two primary methods:

- Javascript snippets of code interacting with web browsers
- Web server log files

Web server logs, common a decade ago, have increasingly become a less popular method of collecting data because most digital marketing today involves more than a website. Web servers generate weblogs when visitors arrive at the site, when visitors request specific pages to be viewed, and when visitors leave the site or simply stop requesting additional information from the server. Web logs' simplicity allows for the basic counting of interactions with the website but remains incredibly limited in terms of their ability to provide detailed information on those visitors. Enter javascript.

Javascript snippets provide a much more versatile means by which to collect data. When visitors arrive on-site or click on links across the internet, the Javascript snippets execute code that collects data about the visitors and interactions and sends that data to a web server to be processed and made available via reports and dashboards. Javascript snippets – or tags commonly referred to – provide a much more robust and rich dataset for analysis. Javascript also allows for the customization of the data collected, and more advanced javascript implementations can send data to multiple recipients – expanding the ability to use different tools. Too many tags can bog down performance, so it is essential to remain thoughtful about which tags to implement and why.

Picking a Tool

Once a digital marketer has a handle on the needed conversions for the marketing campaign, a sense of the KPIs to be used to evaluate that marketing campaign, and an understanding of the best technical approach to deploy to collect the data, a digital analytics program needs a centralized tool or repository to store the data and a shared data source from which to build reports and dashboards. It's time to pick a tool.

The market for digital analytics tools can appear intimidating and complicated to the point where beginning a digital analytics and measurement program feels impossible; like many industries, it's filled with proprietary jargon, complex terminology, and vendors promising to revolutionize business by simply purchasing their products. However, the most prevalent of the analytics tools available out there is free – Google Analytics.

Given Google Analytics's wide availability and no-cost entry point, in most instances, Google Analytics serves as the focal point for an organization's digital analytics efforts. Not only does Google Analytics provide a comprehensive set of reports and analysis resources right out of the box, but a most standard website and digital marketing platforms also have simple integrations with Google Analytics. Furthermore, Google Analytics pairs nicely with Google's small business marketing solutions related to search engine marketing and google directory listings.

More specific information on getting started with Google Analytics can be found here: [Get started with Analytics – Analytics Help] (https://support.google.com/analytics/answer/1008015?hl=en) – https://support.google.com/analytics/answer/1008015?hl=en

Connecting KPIs and Conversions

The easiest way to connect KPIs with Conversions is to use the Goals functionality available in Google Analytics (or similar functionality in related tools). Marketing efforts are defined by configuring Goals, and these marketing efforts help the analytics tool understand and track.

Goals typically take one of the following two forms:

1. Destination Goals – destination goals define a specific page or location a user must reach on the site to trigger the goal. For example, the user must complete a form to get to

a page. The analytics tool itself might not know the user completed the form until the user arrives at the "Thank You" page acknowledging a successful transmission of the information.

2. Action/Event Goals – action, or event goals, define a specific action described on the site as tracked by the analytics tool, such as clicking play on a video or clicking on a link to download a brochure or other type of information. Action events may require additional custom coding to trigger but are worthwhile because one can directly link those actions to outcomes on the site.

The ABCDs of Reading Reports and Dashboards

After connecting the conversion goals and KPIs and configuring the analytics tool to deliver reliable information, it's time to review the data and start making decisions about digital marketing.

The ABCDs of reporting – A for Audience, B for Behavior, C for Content and Conversions, and D for Dollars – provide a simple framework for the types of information available in digital analytics. Marketing investments don't mean much if they're not yielding a monetary return for the business. Analytics reports provide the most helpful feedback in linking those marketing decisions to the financial benefits they intend to deliver.

Note: These are "types" of reports, not necessarily the names of the specific reports themselves. Google Analytics uses these terms very specifically in its tool, and other tools may label tools in the same way they are in Google Analytics.

Audience Reports

Audience reports provide insight into Who visits the site. The reports provide aggregated demographic information. The demographic data in Google Analytics focuses on the age and gender of prospective customers as determined by the advertising those prospects experience while surfing other parts of the internet. Audience reports also provide specific information about visits to the site – are those visits first-time visits, or has this person been to the website in the past?

Audience reports can help provide a sense of the geography from which visitors arrive. Audience data can reveal the technology being used, such as a PC or Mac, with respect to desktop computers, Apple or Android mobile phones, and the different browsers used to access the Internet. Audience members can infer insights about the types of technologies used to experience your marketing and how that could inform marketing investment decisions.

Useful metrics as part of Audience Reporting includes:

- % Male / % Female gender split
- Age Groupings (% users less than 18 years old, 18-24, 25-34, 35-44, 45-54, 55-64, 65 and over)
- % New Users / % Returning Users split
- % Desktop / % Mobile Device split
- % iOS / % Android phone operating system split

Behavior Reports

Behavioral reports dig into the details about how prospects and/or customers engage with marketing campaigns. Behavioral reports include information about campaign tracking, sources of customers/visitors to the website, user flows, customer journeys leading up to abandonment /exists (more on that later) or conversions, and the frequency or depth of engagement with the digital marketing.

Think of behavior reports as How prospects and customers interact with digital marketing. What types of links do they click? What order of pages do they follow while working their way through the site?

Another form of behavioral data is events. Events help marketers track concrete actions users take with the marketing. Events (typically customized depending on the site and marketing materials involved) can include actions users take. Such as: pressing play on a promotional video, interacting with a map or other widget on the site, clicking on a specific link that opens a feedback form, or other important marketing material, etc. Events help marketers understand what resources visitors are most interested in.

Useful metrics as part of the Behavioral Reporting includes:

- Pages per user session
- Average Time on Site (how long does a user stay on the site)
- Top entry or landing pages (the first page users visit when coming to a site)
- Top exit pages (the last page users see just before leaving a

site)

- Top search terms (the terms people search on when using the search functionality of the site)
- Top events/interactions (frequency of actions taken on the site identified as necessary)
- Fastest/Slowest Page Loads (which pages load quickly and which pages slow down the user experience – also possibly the pages which users exit from most often)

Content Reports

A lot of these metrics can feel overwhelming, but there is a model to simplify how to think about this:

Users —> Sessions —> Events —> Content —> Conversions —> Dollars.

In other words, Users create Sessions. In those sessions, users generate events, view content, and ideally convert into prospects or customers based on the actions the digital marketing campaign focuses on. Getting a handle on the types of content that precede these conversion events can provide insight into what unmet needs prospective customers might have and how effective the content associated with the marketing addresses those needs and pushes people further down the marketing path from consideration into a purchase.

Content represents the lifeblood of marketing efforts – the creative, the messaging, the formats used to convey the value proposition.

All of it, to some degree, can be better understood by looking more closely at the content reports available in Google Analytics.

Useful metrics and reports as part of the Content reporting include:

- Top Pages
- Top Directories visited
- Top User Flows

User Flows are the paths users take leading up to a conversion. For example, users may visit the homepage, complete a search for information, watch a video, and then complete a conversion activity all in a single session. Or users might take a more indirect path, visiting multiple times, reading and re-reading certain types of information, perhaps completing a form requesting additional materials, and completing a conversion event after an extended period of time. In any event, that user flows and the paths through the site can inform what is working and what is not working regarding getting marketing messages across to potential customers.

Dollars

There are two ways digital analytics can associate dollars – or revenue – to marketing activities. The first and most apparent reason stems from running e-commerce or similar marketing program where the actual conversion event has a specific dollar amount tied to it. In this instance, every conversion generates revenue for the business. In this direct model, the ROI of the digital marketing investments can be tied to the amount of money generated.

Another way to evaluate digital marketing activities would be to employ an indirect model. In an indirect model, specific actions taken as part of the user flow or journey are given monetary values. By summing up those values across the digital marketing ecosystem, one can make a directional estimate about the effectiveness and efficiency of those marketing investments. For example, let's say one in every ten leads generated by the website becomes a $1,000 customer. One could associate a site conversion goal of form completion to $100. The analytics could determine how much is spent to generate a single lead from your social media and search marketing efforts. While an oversimplification, one could say that if you spend more than $100 to generate a lead and the marketing needs some changes, but spend less than $100 to generate a lead and the marketing is driving positive ROI for the business.

What To Do About Dashboards

Dashboards get a lot of attention. Busy executives don't always have the time to dig into many reports and try to find, quickly and conveniently, the status of digital marketing KPIs. So dashboards fill a need to provide in a single view the most crucial information. Not only can they be visually engaging and compelling, but they can give that business-critical information in real-time. In general, powerful dashboards exhibit the following characteristics:

- Simple, easy to read graphs or numbers
- Real-time, or near real-time, data
- Facilitates the quick identification of exceptions or data points outside of expected performance

A lot of time and effort can be invested in designing and delivering visually compelling and engaging dashboards. A lot of times, dashboards provide a bit of the 'sizzle' associated with analytics efforts. They can showcase essential metrics, and business owners can come to rely on them as part of the processes they follow to run their business.

But most businesses shouldn't just rely on dashboards to get their critical information. Often, dashboards can fail to provide important insight into the progress a company is achieving against its goals. For example, a dashboard might display daily sales and quickly tell a business operating if sales are trending higher or lower than the day or the week prior. But a dashboard, by nature, provides an at-a-glance view of the status of the digital marketing efforts and might not offer a means by which the business owner can determine if sales are progressing as planned against annual targets or allow for the exploration or diving into the data needed to determine if and what changes need to be made to the marketing campaigns. This instance is where having an analyst or someone dedicated to working with the data dig further into the data can be helpful.

Digital marketing is more than a Website

Thus far, much of the discussion has focused on websites and the marketing associated with driving visitors to a website to complete a specific task in the form of a conversion. As an introduction to digital analytics, this simplification is more educational than showcasing the true nature of digital analytics and measurement. In almost every instance, digital marketing campaigns are far more sophisticated than just some marketing designed to drive users to a website. To that end, one can consider some other types of analytics for different aspects of the marketing strategy:

- **Social Media Marketing** – Most influential digital marketing campaigns deliver content and messages across many social media platforms. Tracking across Facebook, Twitter, Instagram, TikTok, YouTube, and others requires a specialized tool that aggregates the data feeds from those platforms into a single location. Tools like SproutSocial and HubSpot do a good job monitoring the social activity across all of the most common social media platforms and provide metrics around a total number of posts, the total number of actual interactions, and provide mechanisms in which you can link those social media posts back to the KPIs.

- **Email Marketing and Lead Generation** – If the marketing relies on email lists or consistent engagement with prospects and customers over email, ensuring that campaign links into emails can help better understand how an audience responds to emails and what types of activities or behaviors they engage in as a result of those emails. Google Analytics provides a robust tracking program by default, and other tools such as HubSpot can help provide additional analytics and insights into a digital marketing email program.

- **Search Engine Optimization** – Every solid digital marketing program includes a strong presence on Google and a reliable positioning on search engine results pages (SERPs) for key terms associated with the business. Because Google also operates Google Analytics, a lot of good information about search campaigns and search can find keywords in Audience reports in Google Analytics. But suppose businesses are interested in taking search marketing efforts to another level. In that case, tools such as SEM Rush and Google Trends can help optimize keyword and search marketing campaigns to deliver results.

- **E-Commerce** – Most e-commerce analytics implementations require additional analytics tagging in conjunction with the software your site uses to operate its digital storefront. Again, Google Analytics does provide a default e-commerce module that can integrate with most common e-commerce software such as Shopify or WooCommerce.

- **Marketing Optimization** – At some point, you might decide digital marketing efforts just aren't living up to expectations, and testing some new ideas or campaigns might be in the cards. Digital analytics provides a solid foundation to test different creative messages and campaign tactics, such as trying out a TikTok channel to reach younger audiences or simply revising your site based on previous analytics insights. Tools like Google Analytics and Optimizely can help digital marketings A/B test ideas and determine which version of a message or campaign tactic works best. In A/B Testing, one message is given to Group A, and another message is given to Group B. The analytics tool then analyzes the interactions of Group A and Group B in terms of their ability to deliver a conversion. Depending on which message wins, the tool can then ensure the appropriate message is given to the relevant audience to ensure the maximum impact of the digital marketing message.

In Conclusion

When it's all said and done, there is no straightforward way to analyze the complexity of human behavior as part of the digital marketing ecosystem available to business managers and owners. In statistical analysis, there is an old saying that "all models are wrong, but some are useful." For digital marketing analytics, there is some wisdom in the expression. No matter how much tracking is put in place, no matter how much control you want over each and every dollar of your marketing spend, determining exactly how each dollar improves your business will be difficult if not potentially frustrating. But that does not mean one should not try to figure some of this out.

Implementing a digital marketing analytics program can help:

- maximize the value from marketing investments
- prioritize those investments and align them with positive business outcomes
- align time and effort associated with marketing decision making to those most impactful on the business strategy

In the long term, companies can grow into more sophisticated approaches. Optimization programs can help marketers test and revise specific messaging and marketing campaigns in real-time.

Matt Booher

Matt Booher brings more than 20 years of experience in managing digital analytics teams and digital measurement projects. Currently, he is working as a Digital Insights and Analytics Director at Scripps Media Inc, Booher leads insights development for local media's broadcasting and digital web sites, apps, and over-the-top (OTT) experiences.

Booher's previous experience includes agency work for respected companies such as P&G, ConAgra Foods, Fifth-Third Bank, Luxottica and Samsung. Booher's journalism background began as a sportswriter at [Fox Sports](http://www.foxsports.com/) and HighWired Sports before moving to DMG Information's educational publisher [Hobsons](https://www.hobsons.com/). At Hobsons, Booher served as director of product development where he leveraged analytics to optimize advertising approaches and publication strategies.

Booher founded the Cincinnati group of Web Analytics Wednesday and has served as a panelist for Online Media, Marketing and Advertising, and American Marketing Association conferences. He graduated from Miami University with a degree in journalism with a focus in interactive media studies and for four years taught a course in web and social media analytics as part of the Armstrong School for Interactive Media Studies at his alma mater.

Matt lives in Cincinnati, Ohio with his wife Melanie and his three, pre-teen, Minecraft and Roblox gamers – McKenna, Madilynn, and Matheson. Matt is a dedicated sports gambler in need of some fresh analytics projects to pay off his debts before he gets kneecapped in a dark Vegas alley.

Connect with Matt:

https://mattbooher.com

https://www.linkedin.com/in/mattbooher/

8.

Pipeline Plumbing

Finding and Fixing the Leaks in Your Sales Pipeline

Kimberlee Vollbrecht, V2 Strategies

The typical B2B company devotes over half its marketing budget to generating leads,[1] yet only 35% have a process to qualify and nurture those leads.[2] That's a lot of potential sales leaking out of your pipeline when you consider:

- 60% of sales take at least 3 months to close[3]
- 80% of purchases happen between the 5th and 12th contact[4]

Potential customers reach out to you for a variety of reasons. Some are ready to buy, but most are looking for information that will help them make the right purchase decision. Staying connected with those knowledge seekers can lead to a 73% increase in conversion.[5]

That's just one example of potential leaks in your sales pipeline. Just like the plumbing in your house, your sales pipeline needs periodic maintenance to identify issues before they cause damaging leaks and backups.

While your sales process may have any number of steps, every prospect goes through three phases: Searching, Comparing, and Deciding. You can identify which phase they're in by the types of questions they ask, and the lead generation prompts that grab their attention.

Searchers are aware they have a problem or unmet need. They're either looking for tools to diagnose their circumstances or options for resolving the issue. Your goals for this stage are two-fold: First, establish your expertise by sharing information, tools, and resources that help your leads understand their situation. Second, present a range of potential solutions in a way that keeps potential buyers in your funnel, and refers the rest to other resources.

Once a lead has identified potential solutions, they need more information to narrow their options. This is a great time to offer case studies, checklists, and comparison charts. Leads who access these types of resources typically have stronger buyer intent. This is your chance to stand out to your ideal leads with examples of how you uniquely meet their needs. It's another opportunity to filter out leads who aren't a good fit by steering them to other resources.

The deciding factors that close the sale will vary by industry, company, and product. They may start with a free trial, then an extended service plan, and finally a limited-time discount offer. Timing is everything. Your offer should start at the first sign of purchase intent, gradually increasing the incentive to act. Look for behavior triggers that help you understand whether those who don't buy within a defined time frame are still interested. You can use behavior tracking (are they still clicking on email links, or visiting your website?), or use survey or quiz tools to get a better perspective on factors influencing their decision timeframe.

While the steps in a nurturing process can seem overwhelming, today's technology makes it easier (and more affordable) than ever to identify where leads are in your sales funnel, qualify prospects, and nurture them through the buying process. You don't need to create an entire funnel's nurture cycle all at once; start with your biggest pain point or opportunity (for example, where do leads get stuck or disappear?), perfect that process, and then reapply what you've learned to other stages.

In the rest of this chapter, we provide examples of four strategies to improve your pipeline plumbing: attract the right leads; weed out the bad fits; nurture and convert prospects; build customer loyalty and referrals.

1: Get more customers like your best customers.

Andy G. has a well-defined niche: IT services for health care providers. By specializing in this highly regulated sector, he can stay on top of regulatory developments that affect his client's unique compliance and operation needs.

Andy quickly gained a small core of loyal customers who contributed the majority of his revenue. In order to grow, he needed to retain these core customers, while bringing in new ones who fit their profile. Toward that end, he developed a lead generation campaign that targeted similar health care providers in a broader geographic region. The campaign was based on Andy's understanding of his target customer decision process:

- Target audience: IT director or manager for large healthcare systems

- How to reach them: articles and advertisements in industry publications; conferences and training seminars; direct mail.

- What drives their decision: quality systems and service, plus strategic insights into their industry that help them stay ahead of potential threats

Despite a variety of high-quality executions, these campaigns had limited success. That meant it was time to take a step back and revisit Andy's assumptions. Fortunately, he already had the resources he needed to get better insights into his target audience: his top customers. They were strong advocates, and happy to meet one-on-one so we could learn more about their decision process.

Note: In order to avoid confirmation bias (where a business owner unconsciously steers the conversation to confirm his assumptions), customer interviews, surveys, and other research tools are best managed by an independent third party. In this case, that approach was priceless. Here's what we learned:

- Andy's current customers were well-acquainted with each other. They were part of a tight-knit peer network, meeting regularly with their counterparts across the region.

- They rarely read industry publications and paid little attention to ads and other marketing materials.

- Their decision to hire Andy's firm was based solely on recommendations from the peer group.

That little bit of customer research was a game-changer for Andy. His pipeline block – getting potential customers to respond to his outreach – wasn't going to be solved with a better marketing plan. He had something far more valuable: the goodwill of his current customers. Once Andy developed a targeted sales strategy, he could rely on allies within their peer network to provide introductions and recommendations.

Marketing can't be effective unless it's linked to a defined sales process and grounded inaccurate customer insights. Marketing plans are designed to get the right information to the right customer at the right time, using the most effective vehicle. The messaging, vehicles, and timing need to be linked to a sales process that will provide a consistent experience across all points of the sales funnel. When marketing isn't designed to qualify and nurture leads to the next step of the sales process, it can end up being a waste of time and resources.

2: Weed Out the Bad Fits

Since Andy's business grew from peer-to-peer referrals, he wasn't concerned about weeding out bad fits. Not everyone has that luxury. In "Angel Customers & Demon Customers: Discover Which is Which and Turbo-Charge Your Stock"[6] Larry Seldon and Geoffrey Colvin used case studies that put a new spin on the 80-20 rule.

It's no surprise that "Angel Customers" refers to the 20% of customers that drive 80% of revenue. "Demon Customers" pose a different challenge. They are a **net cost** to your business, consuming more of your resources in sales team time, returns, and customer service requests than they generate in revenue. Your bottom line will improve when you minimize the number of customers who fit this profile.

How do you weed them out? First, identify the clogs or "friction points" in your sales process – areas where you're spending time or resources, or prospects stagnate. For example, if your "demon customers" constantly negotiate on price, make it clear upfront whether discounts are available. Sometimes sticking points show up late in the sales process when potential customers identify a deal-breaker issue.

Let's look at how one company addressed its top friction points.

Jacob manages marketing and operations for "JCo," a family-owned company with a niche product that represents a once-in-a-lifetime purchase for their target customers. While they had a consistent flow of leads, they had no way to tell which of these were potential buyers. In addition, their CRM system didn't provide insights into where their prospects were in the decision process. This was important, as interested leads could stay in their system for a very long time before they were ready to buy. Once they're ready to act, purchases typically conclude within 30 days.

Qualified leads. JCo generated most of its leads through high-value coupon offers for new subscribers. Their subscriber base kept growing, yet the coupons were seldom redeemed. They needed a better list-building tactic that focused more narrowly on potential buyers.

While qualified leads could stay in their pipeline a long time, their limited inventory turned over quickly. Serious prospects want to find exactly what they're looking for when they are ready to buy and respond well to "don't miss out on your ideal purchase" messaging. Switching to an advanced CRM with better behavior tracking makes it easy to identify when these subscribers move to the "deciding" phase. At that point, the high-value coupon serves as an incentive to complete their purchase.

Address common objections early. JCo's niche product isn't a fit for everyone. Most poor fits are identified quickly and removed from the funnel. A few can move further into the sales process before identifying "deal-breaker" concerns. This can lead to unhappy leads and the occasional poor review. Jacob wanted a better process to guide leads through the qualifying steps so that they don't end up with last-minute objections.

The easiest prospects to weed out were ones looking for a similar product outside of JCo's market, or types of product they don't offer. This was easily addressed by clarifying their market parameters (geography, product type, price range, etc.) early and often.

Next, we developed prompts for each of the potential "deal-breaker" conditions, with links to more detailed information on their website. These topics are covered in their new subscriber welcome emails, social posts, product descriptions, and FAQs on their website.

Lead qualification is a critical part of your sales funnel. Well-designed new lead nurture sequences create a positive first impression with potential buyers while making it easy for poor fits to identify deal-breakers at the start of the process. This helps protect your brand reputation while keeping the door open for future opportunities.

3: Create a Compelling Nurture Experience

Earlier, we described your customer decision process as stages in a sales funnel. Lead nurturing helps move prospects through these stages, by providing relevant information and resources. Email marketing is the primary tool used for nurturing leads, often interspersed with phone calls, chat, and SMS messaging.

You can gauge each prospect's sales-readiness by tracking their interaction with emails, responses to ads, or page visits on your website. When a prospect shows potential interest in the next step, targeted prompts can help move them forward. For example:

- Is this right for you? Click to view case studies or buyer's guides.
- Have questions? Start a chat/schedule a call so we can help.
- Ready to buy? Use this link to learn more about our financing options.

Marketing automation systems make it easy to create and optimize a variety of lead nurture funnels. Companies that take advantage of this technology can yield a 451% increase in qualified leads.[7] Read on for an example of a company that fully automated the first stage of its customer journey.

Growth Partners (GP) offers elite coaching for financial service providers. They offer webinars through partnerships with professional organizations, which generate a steady stream of leads that fit their target profile. Their first challenge was which of these leads are good fits for their entry-level coaching program.

They use a series of finely-honed email marketing campaigns that build a compelling picture of the success available to prospects who become clients, creating a sense of urgency to schedule an initial strategy call. If the initial sequences don't lead to an appointment, prospects move into a slower-paced sequence, culminating in promotions for an annual event. Leads who complete that sequence without scheduling a call are removed from the sales funnel.

All of these sequences are fully automated, enabling their sales team to focus on the initial call with prospects. Separate automation are used to promote call participation and rescheduling if needed.

While this approach sounds complicated, this first-stage prospect automation is critical to GP's business model. Clients who successfully complete the initial curriculum move to advanced coaching programs, leading to a significant number of long-term clients.

4. Don't stop with the (first) sale

Growth Partners has a strong incentive to nurture and encourage their new customers. When new clients have a stellar experience in the entry program, they're more likely to enroll in ongoing coaching services. Without the new client engagement, their investment in lead generation and qualification simply wouldn't pay off. They wouldn't be able to maximize their customer lifetime value.

Two-thirds of businesses understand the importance of calculating customer lifetime value.[8] Despite that recognition, only 29% of brands nurture their existing customers beyond the initial purchase.[9] That means 70% of potential sales leak out of their pipeline. Those customers are still buying related products and services – but they purchase them from someone else.

Email nurture sequences are one of the best ways to keep your customers coming back. Welcome emails, with open rates of over 90%,[10] are an easy and effective way to solidify a strong first impression with new customers, or new purchases by existing customers. That's why over 80% of businesses say email marketing is critical to ongoing customer retention.[11]

Remember those customer insights that helped Andy with the new client acquisition? They're just as important when it comes to driving lifetime value. What does that look like? Here are some examples:

Become Indispensable. We saw earlier that Andy's healthcare customers didn't appreciate his value as a strategic partner until after they started working with him. Working in an industry driven by requests for proposals and competitive bids, doing a great job wasn't enough. Andy needed to help the IT Directors who hired him communicate ongoing value to *their* bosses.

IT services are like air conditioning – no one notices when they're working well, but everyone complains when something goes wrong. Upper management doesn't view "system uptime" as a benefit – it's an expectation. Andy found an opportunity to turn this around by highlighting the benefits of risk prevention: avoided costs from stopping ransomware attacks; maintaining service level requirements by fixing critical issues in 20 minutes instead of the industry standard of 4 hours. By helping his direct customer look good to upper management, Andy can reinforce his value as a strategic business partner.

Anticipate Customer Needs. Cal's technology company provides a range of hardware, software, and managed services to small and mid-sized businesses. New customers come to him with a specific need and often return for related services. Despite periodic communications on his full range of products, Cal would often visit a customer and discover they'd bought something he provided from one of his competitors.

Cal got tired of hearing "if I knew you provided that, I would have bought from you." He needed a better way to anticipate what each customer might need next, and when they were likely to shop for solutions. This would let him target follow-up communications and promotions based on likely customer interest.

We were able to update his current CRM by adding custom fields for Cal's core products and services. The fields identified which items a particular customer might need, which ones they already had, and dates when they might need an update or replacement. These customer insights could be filled in and updated over time, based on conversations by sales and support staff.

Timed reports and saved searches in Cal's CRM make his new "customer intelligence system" a key driver to capture a bigger share of his customers' spending on products and services that he provides.

<u>Out of sight, out of mind</u>. Many residential and commercial businesses provide services that are only needed a few times a year (pest control, HVAC maintenance), or have minimal customer contact after the sale (security, lawn care) while services continue. These businesses frequently have a high level of customer turnover, driven to make a change in response to competitors' offers. Nurture sequences can minimize this turnover by reminding customers of the ongoing value you provide. For example, an HVAC company can

reach out in advance of a heatwave, to reassure customers their AC system will keep them cool.

Remind one-time customers why you're special. Roofing companies typically do one job per customer. While most do neighborhood marketing that leverages a recent roof replacement, that's often the last customer outreach they do. Royal Roofing took a different approach.

Whenever a major storm is predicted, they reach out to all of their past customers, reminding them that their roof is still under warranty. They provide tips to help detect potential issues, offering a free inspection if a customer suspects damage may have occurred. While few past customers take them up on this offer, it's a sure bet that Royal Roofing will be top-of-mind when a friend or neighbor needs a roofing recommendation.

Where will you start?

When I was first exploring email automation systems and didn't know where to start, a helpful salesperson assured me that "Version 1 always outperforms Version None." Just like the proverbial long journey, effective sales pipelines systems are built step-by-step. Each leak you address or friction point you free up gets you closer to your goal.

Before you start, create a clear picture of your destination: what do you want your business to look like in 5 years? What needs to change in your current operations to make that possible? Select one area (save time, increase sales, improve referrals and retention), and identify tools and processes needed to reach your goal. Create a workflow, update your tools if needed, and put your new system to work.

This approach will work for you regardless of whether you're using marketing automation, so long as you consistently follow each step in your workflow. A clearly delineated process will help you identify which steps are working well, and where improvement is needed.

If you're already using sales and marketing technology, there are several reasons to periodically review your system. Service providers continually improve their systems, adding enhancements and new capabilities that can help your business. Customer habits and market dynamics change as well, affecting business strategies and goals. What new capabilities will you need to deliver those goals?

Chances are your current system will be able to get you most of the way to your new goals. When it's time to add new tools like website chat, Messenger marketing, or scheduling apps, it should be easy to find options that sync easily with your existing system. While you might be tempted to use all-in-one solutions, most businesses get better results by picking individual tools that best meet their needs.

If you're not sure where to start, we'd be happy to help. Reach out on LinkedIn (https://www.linkedin.com/in/kimvollbrecht/), or use the scheduling button on our website (v2strategies.com) to set up a quick call. There's nothing to lose – and you may qualify for one of our free small business strategy sessions.

Notes

1. Startup Bonsai: 30+ Lead Generation Statistics, Facts and Trend for 2021, https://startupbonsai.com/lead-generation-statistics/

2. Invespcro: The Importance of Lead Nurturing – Statistics and Trends, https://www.invespcro.com/blog/lead-nurturing/
3. Rivkin: 42 Sales Statistics that will Help Improve Your Selling, https://www.rikvin.com/blog/42-sales-statistics-that-will-help-improve-your-selling/
4. IRC Sales Solutions: Sales Follow-Up Statistics and Process – The Power of Follow-Ups https://ircsalessolutions.com/insights/sales-follow-up-statistics
5. Aberdeen: How to Define Market Needs to Align Content Effectively, https://www.aberdeen.com/cmo-essentials/define-market-needs-align-content-effectively/
6. Angel Customers and Demon Customers, Discover Which is Which, and Turbo-Charge Your Stock, Kindle Edition https://www.amazon.com/Angel-Customers-Demon-Discover-Turbo-Charge/dp/1591840074
7. Company Acquisition vs. Retention Costs (Investpcro)://www.business2community.com/infographics/marketing-automation-by-the-numbers-infographic-0342287#%21rFqTU
8. Clevertap: Customer Lifetime Value: What it is and How to Calculate It https://clevertap.com/blog/customer-lifetime-value/
9. Demand Gen: 2016 Lead Nurturing Study https://www.demandgenreport.com/resources/reports/2016-lead-nurturing-benchmark-study/
10. Campaign Monitor: How Effective are Welcome Emails https://www.campaignmonitor.com/resources/infographics/how-effective-are-welcome-emails/
11. Emarketer: Email Marketing is a Double Win for Customer Acquisition, Retention https://www.emarketer.com/Article/Email-Marketing-Double-Win-Customer-Acquisition-Retention/1014239

Kimberlee Vollbrecht

Kimberlee Vollbrecht, President of V2 Strategies and marketing tech evangelist, has a simple approach to sales funnel design: if it doesn't work for you…it doesn't work.

Her demand-focused solutions work because they're based on each company's unique customer insights, fit their sales and marketing process, and support longer-term goals and objectives. They've helped an independent caterer double sales from her email newsletter, an IT services firm set up a customer-intelligence system to support inside sales, and a coaching enterprise automate the prospect-to-satisfied-client journey.

When she's not providing clients with success solutions, Kim loves time spent with her family and friends, nature walks with her rescue dog Roxie, and activities that center on solving mysteries or putting puzzle pieces together. As a child, she'd start jigsaw puzzles from the inside out, creating a picture from individual pieces that naturally fit together. That ability to see connections first, and then assemble the picture, has helped her successfully build coalitions, shift opinions, and drive sales throughout her career.

Connect with Kimberlee:

http://v2strategies.com/

https://www.linkedin.com/in/kimvollbrecht/

9.

Relationship Networking and Marketing

Katie Scanlon, BNI Southwest Ohio and Northern Kentucky

My "Why"

Everyone has their story on how they got into their business or career. How it started, how they got there. Their "Why." Was it something they knew from the time they were a child, something they learned in school with education or learned over time? For me, it was like a 100-mph fastball coming straight for me…and I had a choice. A choice to move out of the way and let it fly right past me or step out in front and catch it.

Unbeknownst to me, my "WHY," and what I would do with my life, were in front of me for over 16 years. My husband Brennan had taken over his father's franchise business called BNI in 2013. I watched and listened throughout my life with my husband, as he ran his business like his 2nd family. He ran it with passion and pride, with sincerity, and with integrity. He loved what he did, and it showed. Everyone he met became his friend, and he built so many long-lasting relationships, and I didn't know it at the time. Still, behind the scenes, he was teaching me about building unique, trustworthy relationships with business professionals who would later become some of my best friends. He would say, when asked what he did for a living, "I help people create referrals for life by helping them to create the richest relationships of their lives." And He lived up to that every day.

In 2019, my world came crashing down around me when my husband unexpectedly passed away. I was now the new owner of our BNI franchise here in the Cincinnati/Northern Kentucky area. Not only had my whole world changed personally, but I also had two options: keep the business or sell. I could stay in my comfortable little box at my job of 16 years OR…I could run forward, embracing this new gift that the world handed to me. Ultimately, I chose to step out into the unknown. My "WHY" is to carry my husband's and his father's legacy into the future, to keep BNI here in the Cincinnati area, where it helped (and continues to help) so many businesses around the community.

What is BNI?

Let me take a step back a moment – back to 1985 when BNI all started. What is BNI? A man by the name of Dr. Ivan Misner founded a network called Business Network International. His story began when he was working on his own growing business, and a thought came to him: "Of all the kinds of business that came to me, the best business came in by referral. We needed a networking system designed to generate the largest possible number of high-quality referrals from as many sources as possible for the mutual benefit of all and do it positively. And to avoid competition, only one member per professional category would be allowed." (SITE REFERENCE GIVERS GAIN by Dr. Ivan Misner). Thus, BNI was born and slowly formed into what we now know it is today. Today, BNI is a global company in 70 countries. It's the largest Referral Networking organization with 283K international members. BNI's mission is to help members increase their business through a structured, positive, and professional referral marketing program that enables them to develop long-term, meaningful relationships with quality business professionals.

What sets BNI apart from most networking groups is the structure of the organization of each chapter, having only one person per professional classification and our Core values. The main one is Givers Gain. The Givers Gain philosophy is to help others succeed and get quality referrals, which would, in turn, then end up helping you be successful as well. Dr. Misner's words are, "we reasoned the most effective way to show new and prospective members how powerful the groups could be was to give them as many good referrals as possible, as quickly as possible. This meant that each member must go into the organization with one question in mind: What can I do to help other members?"

Relationships Start with Trust

For any type of relationship to work, whether personal or professional, and refer to one another, you have to know, like, and trust them. A good example of this can be seen related to cold calling. Have you ever had to cold call to get business? How many times have you been on the receiving end of a cold call? Did you say, "Yes, I don't know you, but I will buy your product right now, let me get my credit card to pay you?" That doesn't happen very often. I am not saying cold calling doesn't have its advantages. It certainly does for some businesses, but if you are anything like me, I have never been comfortable with doing or receiving. I would prefer to stay away if possible. That is where referral marketing comes in.

Building relationships to help get referrals helps you not have to ever cold call again to get customers because you have a group of people who learn to know, like, and trust you and will go out and do your marketing for you every day! Here in BNI, we have a chapter every week filled with our marketing team. Think of all the time, effort, and money you save by having your own business in front of 20-40 people every week.

Accountability is the way to get someone to know, like, and trust you. Every week, we show up to our meetings to showcase our investment in our business and others,' we see the people we are doing business with. Everyone holds each other accountable. As we learn more and more about those in our chapter, the relationship starts to grow; with that, we begin to trust those around us. Forming these relationships is the essential part. Going out for coffee, meeting for a happy hour…these are the ways you learn about each other. Once that relationship and trust have formed, you feel comfortable referring this business partner to family and friends.

Relationships take time to grow. Most experts say around six months to start feeling comfortable with referring someone to someone else, and they are based on specific "requirements." In BNI, we call this VCP – Visibility, Credibility, and Profitability. Let's break this down: Visibility is being seen. In BNI, this means showing up to your meetings, being present. Are you accountable? I learned another great way of being seen and staying visible is following up with a quick phone call, email, or yes, even a handwritten card. Sending a handwritten note is one of my favorite ways of being seen because who does not love getting a piece of mail that is not junk mail or a bill, am I right? The follow-up process is called the 24/7/30 system. Send a handwritten note or email within 24 hours, connect with them on social media within seven days – i.e., LinkedIn, and within 30 days, reach back out for another face-to-face or Zoom meeting.

Credibility comes once you are Visible. People know who you are and what you do. And they know you are good at what you do. They TRUST you. Profitability comes once you are visible and credible. You start to get a profitable return on the time and money you invested in your relationships or other business. In BNI, we have compared the VCP process to an ATM. You cannot get money out if you have a zero account balance, so there is nothing to get out of the ATM unless you deposit money into your account first. You must put something into your relationship before being able to get anything out. By using visibility and credibility, your relationships will continue to grow, Trust will be formed, and you will hopefully become more profitable – they all go hand in hand.

Building Relationships via Zoom

In 2020, my world changed again, but this time, it was the whole world. I was not alone. It changed whether we liked it or not. We were forced to change the way we looked at the business and how we did business. For an in-person networking group, this was not going to be good…or so I, and many others, thought. So many things were running through my head. How was BNI going to stay in business? How was I going to keep my franchise? How do you still form personal and professional relationships with people if you cannot see them or be with them in person? How will we get to know one another if we do not see or feel the energy of those people we are meeting with? Face to face, in person, is how it has always been done.

But…BNI was ready for the change. Within a month, all of our chapters globally were up and running via the new way of doing things – Zoom. Most of the time, people resist change; we do not like it; it's human nature not to want to change the way you have been doing something or are comfortable doing it. However, if we wanted to keep doing business during a very tumultuous time, this was the only way forward.

BNI saved many companies from failing. How? Members had relationships and a network of people around them who cared for them and knew them and did business with them. Their fellow chapter members were there to step up. I heard countless stories of members whose companies were not faring well with the pandemic, and others stepped up and helped them by buying Gift Cards, using member businesses more often, and by marketing their business for them even more. It warmed my heart how so many people came together for their BNI chapter family members.

Keeping the relationships going throughout the year 2020 was not always an easy task. We found new innovative ways to do business, to network. Happy Hours over Zoom, Online Speed networking events, check-ins, phone calls, and handwritten cards through the mail in order to keep those relationships going.

Here is one of those examples: Chapter member Josh was a newer print and vinyl wrap shop owner and had been in BNI for just over a year. His business was growing every month until like many other businesses, everything came to a halt during the pandemic. His main marketing tactic was stopping by a business to introduce himself and that stopped overnight. The one thing that kept his business afloat was the great relationships made in BNI with people who are caring and want to give. BNI helped him pivot the way he did business and who he marketed to, and he is now surpassing his business numbers from before the pandemic. He quoted, " There is no doubt I would have no longer been open if it wasn't for the great relationships, referrals, and friendships I got from my BNI chapter."

Relationships are essential in our lives and are necessary for our businesses. It can be hard work to keep relationships going. You have heard it before "Net-WORK." It can take time and effort, but it's so worth it for the outcome. Just remember to think, "How would I like to be treated by others? What would it take for me to trust them to do business?" They are asking themselves these same questions, so make sure you are practicing what you preach. Hold yourself accountable to become the best-referrable business partner you can be. You will not be disappointed in the results.

BNI members have become my second family; they are who I go to for advice, they are who I look to, to find businesses and referrals that I can trust & they are ones I know I can call on whenever I need them. These are the relationships I want in my life as I continue to move forward.

Consider these questions:

- Who do you want to be a part of your life?
- Are you being that person for someone else?

Relationships are powerful and can change your life personally and professionally for the better! In the words of my late husband, Brennan Scanlon, "Help people create referrals for life by helping them to create the richest relationships of their lives."

Katie Scanlon

Katie Scanlon is the Executive Director for BNI (Business Network International) of Southwest OH Northern KY.

BNI SWONKY (as it's nicknamed locally) was started in the Greater Cincinnati area by Katie's Father in Law, Geof Scanlon, in 1994. In 2014, her husband Brennan took over the family business. After losing Brennan in 2019, Katie left her 16-year career at Fidelity Investments to take on the business. She has since made it her personal goal to carry Geof & Brennan's legacy into the future by continuing to help small businesses grow through referrals and create long-lasting relationships through BNI.

She is part of the Four Leaf Family Foundation, a non-profit which was started in memory of Brennan's brother Brady Scanlon, who passed away in 2005. Proceeds raised are used to assist local families adversely affected by Melanoma or other cancers, as well as other local charities.

She has a bachelor's degree in Business Administration with a minor in Marketing from Northern Kentucky University. She currently resides in Ft. Wright, KY with her 2 cats Penny & Wilson. When she is not working, you can find her enjoying the outdoors, traveling, or reading a book with a nice glass of wine.

Connect with Katie:

https://bniswonky.com

https://www.linkedin.com/in/katie-scanlon-95459873/

10.

One Chapter, One Bio and A Headshot

How to Market Your Business with a Multi-Author Book

Jodi Brandstetter, Influence Network Media

The opportunity to share my insights on how to market you and your business in this multi-author book is amazing. I get to provide my knowledge and expertise on how a chapter in a multi-author book can be your vessel to your professional career and business aspirations. And I get to benefit from being in a multi-author book myself and putting together my own marketing plan to promote me and my business. It is almost like I am writing this to myself as well as to you. By the end of this chapter, you will understand the benefits of being a business expert, business owner, and author of a multi-author book.

Being able to become an author with just one chapter is a powerful thing. Around 2,500 words, and then "author" is now next to your name. A book is out there for people to purchase and that book can become a bestseller. How incredible is that?!

The questions for a business owner are:

"Why become an author?"

"How can becoming an author drive sales or increase market share or land a new client?"

A book itself cannot do this. It's up to the author to create the opportunities with the book.

Before this question is answered, understanding the benefits of a multi-author book versus a solo book, in general, is needed. Not only does an author just need to write one chapter versus ten chapters, but a multi-author book gives the author the ability to collaborate with other experts in the same or similar field(s). Collaboration of the book equals tapping into each other's networks. It can also bring more credibility to each author involved in the book project. And it can help each author with building a strong business and brand.

Branding yourself as the expert and showing credibility with a book, can launch a business to a new level. Here are 3 ways to use a multi-author book to successfully market you and your business.

1. Your Chapter's Content

2,500 words may sound easy and seem like something you can do in your sleep. But, for a multi-author book to drive success to and for your business, your content is important. Think of your chapter as the marketing material for your business.

What type of services do you offer?

How can you highlight those services within the chapter?

The content you decide to write in your chapter will be content you will talk about all the time. Ensure that the content is around the services that you want to be doing. This is not the time to try something new or talk about services you do not want to do.

When I wrote my book, "Hire by Design," I wanted to highlight the methodology that I wanted to use with my consulting business. I focused on areas I felt confident that I could help businesses with and had case studies to back up my ideas.

Who is your target audience?

What do they need from you?

Understanding your ideal client or customer and speaking to those individuals will help attract the right clients to your business. Ensuring that you are providing a solution that they need will also help them in reaching out to you. A "Reader Persona" should mirror your "Customer Persona."

My reader persona for "Hire by Design" was small to midsize business leaders in science, technology, engineering, and manufacturing. I made sure that my stories and my content was appealing to this audience.

By knowing what you want to write about and who you are writing to will ensure the content in your chapter is able to market you as the expert and your business as the preferred provider.

2. Connect with your Reader Persona (aka client persona) – Pre-launch, Launch, and Post-Launch

It is important for an author to connect with the ideal readers even before the book launches. Letting them know that the book is coming, providing a sneak peek into the chapter, answering questions, and getting insights from the readers will help with the success of your chapter and your book.

Authors who are available to their readers make the book experience more appealing. Allowing the readers to join the author on the writing journey gives the reader the "behind the scenes" insight and knowledge of the book.

Getting the reader's insights on different topics lets them share the writing journey with the author. This also ensures that the chapter will resonate with the readers.

Providing information on the other authors of the book to the readers helps validate the book and gives readers more connection with the full book. It is like painting a picture. The focal point of the painting is the chapter and the background of the painting is the other chapters in the book. Put the focal point and background together and the painting comes to life.

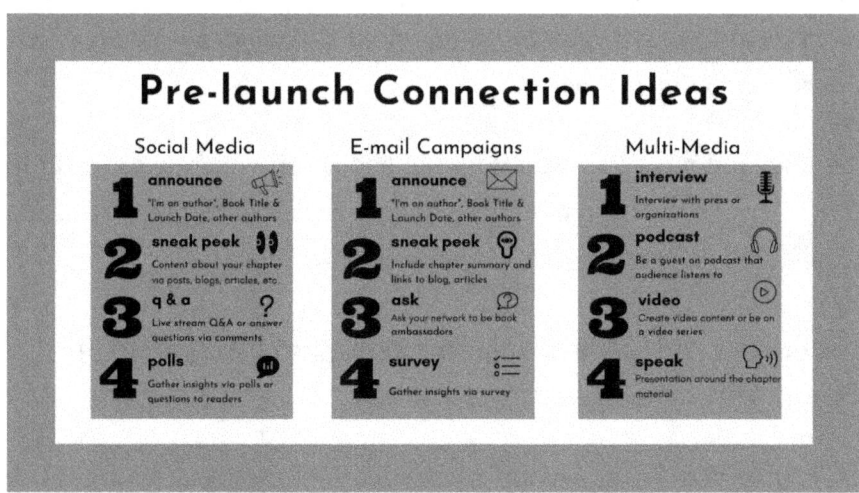

The day of the book launch is the time to keep the readers up-to-date and informed on the success of the book. There are milestones that a book hits on launch date; from being a ranked new release to reaching bestseller status. Keep your readers updated on when the book hits each milestone. The excitement of the day pushes readers to become ambassadors for the book. Encouraging their network to help you, the author, helps you hit these milestones.

Once the milestones are hit, celebrate with the authors, readers and everyone who helped get the book on the bookshelf. This can be via virtual networking events, to book signing events, to a launch party. Enjoy the success and the book launch….you deserve it!

It is important to note that the work is not done once the book launches. Continuing to connect with readers and potential new readers will keep the book alive.

Some ideas to do this are:

- Interview a reader and ask about their experience reading the book and takeaways s/he has implemented.
- Live or Recorded Chat with the other authors of the book.
- Ask for recommendations and reviews and highlight the ones received
- Celebrate milestones
    - The day you get your paperback copy
    - First book signing

- Pictures of readers with their copy of the book
- Anniversaries of the book launch
- Showcase media appearances
- Content around the writing journey (what you learned, what you would do differently, etc.)
- Book = Business Card
  - Share books with clients, and potential clients, as a gift or as your business card
  - Create a bookmark to include in the book with your contact information

Connecting with readers keeps you in the spotlight and provides you with the ability to serve your audience. The more connections made, the more opportunity for you and your business.

3. Re-Purpose Chapter

Continuing to use the content from your chapter in different ways can be a simple way to brand yourself as the expert and highlight the products/services you offer to clients.

Here are a few examples of how to repurpose your chapter.

Continue to Write

Your chapter can evolve into more content. In fact, your chapter can evolve into your own book. Your chapter can be a chapter in your book, or you can expand the chapter into several chapters and voila you have a book!

The content of your chapter can become a series of articles or blogs. The articles can be provided to industry-specific websites or publications. Your blog can be monetized with sponsored content. The articles and blogs can be used for email campaigns or newsletters.

Content marketing is a great way to keep you and your business in front of your audience.

Freebies – everyone loves them!

Email marketing is still one of the best ways to connect with your clients and potential clients. Finding ways to get new email addresses can help build that email list. And people love free stuff!

Using your chapter as a freebie for potential clients is a great way to repurpose your chapter. You can package the chapter like an e-book, audiobook, or just use the pdf version.

And this is a nice freebie so you can probably ask for more than just an email address.

Videos are all the rage

There is so much information out there about why video content is better than text content. People are drawn to a video more than they are to text. Why do you think TV and movies are more popular than reading a book? Because it is easier to watch something engaging than it is to read!

Taking the time to repurpose your chapter into videos will increase your audience. Also, creating short video/audiograms about the book can increase the number of people who click on your content and then eventually, hopefully, they'll buy the book.

Monetize Your Chapter through Courses

Creating a course that gives the reader the ability to learn from you is a great way to monetize your chapter. The course can be online, in person, or both. Just remember to design the course for your ideal reader/client. Figure out the best way to serve the reader/client based on their challenges.

Monetize Your Chapter through Speaking

It is amazing how people see you differently after you become an author.

I had been on the speaking circuit for several years before I became an author. And I just could not break into getting paid to speak. That is until I became an author. Once I had "author" by my name, I was getting organizations and event planners left and right asking me about speaking and about my speaker fee.

*Even organizations that I was a member and volunteer of finally saw me as a speaker. I had been trying to speak at one organization for years for free. I did not get anywhere until I was a bestselling author. And guess what? They did not get my services for free. I got **paid**.*

*Same story with a conference. I had raised my hand for several years to speak and always got the "thanks but no thanks" email. Finally, I got a call about speaking this year and not only did I get to speak but I got **paid**!*

The credibility of a book helps organizations and companies see you in a different light. They can now rationalize why they should pay you for your services including speaking.

Take the time to create presentations around your chapter and start marketing yourself as a speaker. And always ask about a speaker fee. If you do not ask, you will never know. And it is completely up to you if you want to speak for free or only when you get paid.

Put It All Together

By branding yourself and your business cohesively through all these channels, you will surely reap the rewards. Consistent marketing with the same voice, look, and feel helps your audience to remember who you are and what you do.

Create a chapter that gives you the ability to create a course, video series, and speaking opportunities. You will touch a larger audience of your ideal reader/client. By using the same content and message, it makes your life easier when it comes to marketing.

Yes, writing a chapter, launching the book, and repurposing your chapter is not easy. But if you do it right, you will see the return on your investment. It can be worth your time and energy.

And hey…who doesn't want "author" and, better yet, "bestselling author" next to their name?

Example Marketing Plan from a Multi-Author Book:

Marketing Plan for INM with Marketing Fusion

Reader/Client Persona:
Small Business Owners within the professional services industry looking for ways to promote themselves & businesses.

Marketing Fusion launches January 2022.
Marketing Plan starts in December and continues through 2022.

Chapter's Content
focus on discussing how a SMB can utilize a multi-author book opportunity and provide stories to paint the picture.

Connect with Readers
Pre-launch: Share content via social media and e-mail campaigns including announcement, Q&A, polls & sneak peek. Connect with authors and create content about book. Pitch SMB focus podcast for guest appearances. Create presentation that compliments the chapter.

Launch: Keep audience inform on book achievements and celebrate with network and authors on successes.

Post-launch: Encourage readers to recommend and review. Highlight achievements for me and other authors. Pitch media appearances around marketing your business as an author.

Re-purpose Content
- Write a book around being a business expert author
- Pitch blog and articles for websites/associations around SMBs.
- Provide E-book & Audio Version of my chapter as a freebie
- Short Videos on Marketing Your Business as Author (YouTube) monthly
- Focus on obtaining new authors for new Multi-Author Book Courses
- Pitch Presentation to local and national associations and chambers

Jodi Brandstetter

Jodi believes every business expert has a book inside of them. As a Recruiting expert and bestselling author, Jodi understands how a book can open doors to promote your expertise as well as your business.

Her bestselling book, Hire by Design, is the playbook for strategic and intentional, human-focused talent acquisition. Her book is a perfect mix of "writing the rules," while also being delivered in an approachable and enjoyable way. It is the book that meets business needs in today's world.

Jodi has 20 years of HR and recruiting experience and is certified in design thinking. Her expertise in recruiting and retaining top talent is a game-changer for small and midsize companies in science, manufacturing, engineering, and tech.

Jodi is the CEO of:

- Lean Effective Talent Strategies – a talent acquisition consulting firm
- Talent Acquisition Evolution – a community for recruiting professionals to connect, learn, and work together
- Influence Network Media – a media company that provides production, publication and promotion services for business experts to write bestselling books.

Jodi lives outside of Cincinnati, OH with her husband, Ron, daughter, Lena, and her fur-children – Dali and Monet.

Connect with Jodi:

https://authors.influencenetworkmedia.com

https://linkedin.com/in/jodibrandstetter

Conclusion

We are blessed to have these Marketing Leaders share their expertise and knowledge with us. Through coaching, training, writing, and cheering, they are now all authors! The INM team has enjoyed being part of these authors' writing journey and we look forward to seeing their continued success.

Each chapter of Marketing Fusion contains unique content and differentiating approaches. Business leaders desire to strengthen of brand and differentiation from competitors. In today's world, it's hard to get all of this without hiring different employees who possess the width and depth of experience to operate in all these facets. This is where Marketing Fusion comes into play. Our authors have provided a valuable toolbox to help level up or supplement current Marketing efforts and overall Marketing Strategy. As leaders assess their current plan and determine where gaps exist – we are confident this book can fill those gaps and spur ideas for improvement.

If you are inspired and thirsting for more (or in need of help to get it accomplished!), then we encourage you to reach out to our thought leaders for additional help, coaching or consulting. Let's drive your marketing efforts forward in a positive and innovative way. Learn from experts. Take what resonates and cast aside the rest. Work smarter, not harder. Utilizing Marketing Fusion expertise will surely set your business apart from others.

Thank you for supporting these amazing marketing experts and authors – and their book Marketing Fusion. We are excited to have a Fusion series of books launching. These books all support business leaders: Talent, Marketing, Leadership, People, and Sales. Visit Amazon to get the complete set (Talent Fusion 2021, with the others coming soon!).

And – if writing a chapter sounds like something you'd enjoy doing, please connect with us.

~ Melanie Booher, President of INM

Melanie Booher

Melanie Booher is a veteran business leader who strives to make the world better – one workplace at a time. With 20+ years of business experience, Melanie develops leaders across 3 dimensions: as individual development, by inspiring and guiding leaders to find and share their voice, as team development, by harnessing the power of habit to influence people, and as organizational improvement, by spurring change to create workplace cultures that THRIVE. She is the President of Influence Network Media, Chief People Officer of PEOPLEfirst Talent & Retention Consulting, and creator of the THRIVE^{TM} Model, *Cards for Culture©*, and the *Conscious Culture Certified Coach* program. Melanie believes that great cultures represent a collective commitment that is bigger than any one of us. She inspires others to create a pay-it-forward legacy – leaving the world a better place than we found it. One good person, one game plan, one great work culture at a time. Join the movement – knowing that together we THRIVE^{TM}!

Her books *Conscious Culture* and *Talent Fusion* launched in 2021. Melanie lives outside of Cincinnati, OH with her husband and 3 children.

Connect with Melanie:

https://authors.influencenetworkmedia.com/

https://www.linkedin.com/in/melanie-booher/

About Influence Network Media

Influence Network Media

We provide publishing & promotional services to business experts who want to become authors.

A media company that provides publishing and promotional coaching and services to authors who write non-fiction books around people in business. Founded by Jodi Brandstetter and Melanie Booher, Influence Network Media is a one-stop shop to ensure your book is a best seller and authors are able to use their book as a vessel to their career success.

We provide *courses, coaching,* and *VIP concierge* services to help authors write, publish and promote their book.

Our offerings include:

- Multi-author Book Opportunities where you only need one chapter, bio and headshot to become an Amazon Best Selling Author!

- Solo Book Opportunities where we provide the tools (Courses), the guides (Coaching) or everything but the writing of the book (VIP Concierge).

MEET THE TEAM

Jodi Brandstetter, CEO

Jodi, CEO, believes a book can push your career to the next level. It did for her. Her bestselling book, Hire By Design, open doors to paid speaking gigs, podcast appearances, and an increase in consulting business.

Melanie Booher, President

As the President of INM, Melanie helps grow the brand through business development, networking, and marketing. Lead with heart, find your voice, and together we THRIVE!

Alexandra Glossner, Publishing Manager

As the Publishing Manager at Influence Network Media, Alex is happy to take her skills as a former English teacher to the publishing and marketing world. Having been in education for almost a decade, she has a focus and passion for writing in particular. Alex hopes that her experience and love of writing serve to be a great support for all who wish to seek the expertise of Influence Network Media!

CONTACT INFO:

Publishing@LETSCincy.com

https://Authors.InfluenceNetworkMedia.com

Business Fusion Book Series

Collaborative Book Series

A Book Series Dedicated to Small to Midsize Businesses and their Success

 Launched August 2021

 Launched January 2022

Coming Soon:

Summer 2022   Fall 2022   Winter 2023

Women of Business Book Series

Collaborative Book Series

Women of Business

A Book Series for the
Future Generations of Women Leaders

Coming Soon!

Influence Network Media Multi-Author Book Services

Multi-Author Book Opportunity

Want to be an author but do not have time to write 30k word book?

 You can become an author with just 3k word chapter with our multi-author book opportunity!

Looking for a cost effective way to become an author?

 A multi-author book is affordable and we provide all the training and tools to become an author!

Do you want to become an Amazon Bestselling author?

 We guarantee bestselling status with our multi-author book opportunity!

You write your chapter, provide bio and headshot and WE do the rest!

- Training
- Book Cover Design
- Editing & Formatting
- Book Launch Strategy
- Marketing Materials
- Produce & Publish

Influence Network Media

Book Smarts Business Podcast

Short on time but big on growth? Then the Book Smarts Business Podcast is the podcast for you – the experienced, business professional who loves to listen to podcasts and read business books all in an effort to learn more about his/her profession, become an expert in their field, or maybe even become an entrepreneur down the road!

In 15 minutes, you will learn more about the expert authors, gain amazing insights and knowledge from their unique expertise, as well as the ins & outs about their book, and why they decided to write their book!

For a potential author, Book Smarts Business Podcast provides an avenue for business authors to showcase their expertise and book, and gain more readers for their book!

https://booksmartsbusiness.buzzsprout.com/

www.ingramcontent.com/pod-product-compliance
Lightning Source LLC
Chambersburg PA
CBHW071451220526
45472CB00003B/759